CRICKET'S BLACK DOG

ANDREW MURTAGH

CRICKET'S BLACK DOG

THE STORY OF DEPRESSION AMONG CRICKETERS

pitch

First published by Pitch Publishing, 2025
1

Pitch Publishing
9 Donnington Park,
85 Birdham Road,
Chichester, West Sussex,
PO20 7AJ

www.pitchpublishing.co.uk
info@pitchpublishing.co.uk

A CIP catalogue record is available for this book from the British Library.

ISBN 978 1 83680 120 7

Typesetting and origination by Pitch Publishing

MIX
Paper | Supporting responsible forestry
FSC® C010615

Printed and bound on FSC® certified paper in line with our continuing commitment to ethical business practices, sustainability and the environment.

Printed and bound in India by Thomson Press

Contents

This book is dedicated to Terry Blake, a fellow depressive whose idea it was and whose help and support have been unstinting throughout.

No company's more hateful than your own
You dodge and give yourself the slip; you seek
In bed or in your cups from care to sneak
In vain, *the black dog* follows you and hangs
Close to your flying skirts with hungry fangs.

(Horace, Roman poet)

What will you do to keep away *the black dog* that worries you at home?

(Samuel Johnson, poet, critic, lexicographer,
writing to a friend in 1783)

Preface

In every cliché, every commonplace, there is more than a grain of truth. How about these:

> 'Let me state the obvious. Illegal immigration is … illegal.'
> *President John Kennedy.*

> 'Whoever said the pen is mightier than the sword never encountered automatic weapons.'
> *General Douglas MacArthur.*

> 'I notice that anyone who is for abortion has already been born.'
> *President Ronald Reagan.*

> 'Open the door before entering. Thank you.'

> 'Date of birth?' '5th July.' 'What year?' 'Every year.' (In an English courtroom)

> *Caution – Cricket Balls.* (Affixed to the fence of our local cricket club)

> 'Creekit – it's a foony old game.'
> *Sir Geoffrey Boycott.*

Yet Boycott is right; cricket *is* a funny old game. Let me recount an incident when I was teaching at Malvern

College. I was watching from the Senior Bank the first XI attempting to chase down a target on a sunny afternoon. A German pupil, who was in my English class, sidled up and joined me on the bench.

'Good afternoon, Sir. Are you enjoying ze cricket?'

The German pupils at the College were possessed of impeccable manners. I assured him that I was, but my mood could change at any moment should we lose a wicket. He pondered that fact before asking a very obvious question.

'Tell me, Sir. Who is vinning? Is it ze team in vite?'

That would take a lot of explaining, I thought, but my attention was distracted by a crass piece of running between the wickets that almost resulted in the loss of a wicket.

'Vere are zey going?' cried my German friend.

'Tea time,' I said.

He looked at me incredulously and then nodded his head as if the scales had fallen from his eyes.

'Of course. Only ze English could stop in the middle of a game for a cup of tea.'

Later, on reflection, I had to admit that he had a point. Boycott is right. Cricket is a funny old game.

***

Ergo, it stands to reason that the game must be played by funny old people. As professional players, plying our trade the length and breadth of the country in the County Championship, we considered ourselves neither old nor funny. In fact, we were deeply earnest and totally committed to the game. We were professionals. We were paid to perform. Our very livelihood depended on how well we played. There was no messing about. There were of course lighter moments, when what had occurred was indeed amusing, but cricket was a serious business, taken seriously.

We soon learned the ropes: punctuality;concentration; dedication; practice; clean kit; attention to detail; etiquette; personal responsibility. Anybody who didn't was soon sent on his way.

It's only when you stop playing that the essential absurdity of what you have been doing slowly sinks in. Once retired, all those overs bowled, all those irresponsible shots, all those hours spent in the field, count for nothing. They merely remain as footnotes, old scorecards on dusty shelves, or nowadays, entries in cricket archives on the internet, gradually becoming no more than fraying memories. What was all that about, you ask yourself. Why did I get so upset when I bowled that loose half-volley? It's all in the past.

In one sense, this loss of identity, of *raison d'être*, is shared by all sportsmen and women when Anno Domini catches up with them. Necessarily, retirement, either forced or chosen, happens at a much earlier age than in other professions. All right, Stanley Mathews played his last game for Stoke City when he was 50 and Wilfred Rhodes played his last Test match when he was 52 but they were exceptional, and both played in different eras. There are cricketers playing today who are seemingly able to resist the passage of time – my own nephew, Tim Murtagh, was still bowling for Middlesex in his 42nd year as was Jimmy Anderson, but by and large a cricketer's career ends in his 30s. Remember that famous song by The Byrds that was a massive hit in 1965?

> 'To everything there is a season and a time to
> every purpose under heaven.
> A time to be born and a time to die ...'

The lyrics were taken verbatim from the Book of Ecclesiastes in the King James Bible. James I was a Scotsman. It is unlikely he had ever heard of cricket (though he did play golf) but if he had, he might well have accepted the analogy to our summer game.

For some, the wrench away from the game is cruel, the fear of which prompts a desperate hanging on, a raging against the dying of the light, a holding out for one last contract. This never seemed to me to be good for the health of the game. When I was playing, I could name dozens of players who could still 'do a job' but their best days were behind them, and they were clogging up the pathway for younger talent. Let me give you an example. In the Hampshire v Australia tour match of 1975 Peter Sainsbury and I were engaged in a desperate rearguard action in our second innings to prevent an Australian victory (in which we were successful, I dare to point out). Earlier in the day, Barry Richards and David Turner had been felled by Jeff Thomson, both retired hurt. It was not a cakewalk; it was distinctly unpleasant out there. Not because Thommo was directing missiles at us – he was more concerned with his run-up and no-ball problems – but on account of the continuous bile directed at us by one Ian Chappell. 'Have you ever been spoken to like that on a cricket pitch?' Sains enquired of me. I admitted that even the bully at school had seemed like a pussy cat in comparison. I have to admit that Chappell's animosity was directed more at Sainsbury than at me. Afterwards, I asked of Richards, our captain for the day, what Sainsbury had done in another life to upset the Australian captain. His answer was educative. 'Peter Sainsbury encapsulates all that Chappell *hates* about English cricket, players that hang on to their jobs by hook or by crook, thus filling up places in the team that should be taken by younger players.' I felt that this was a bit harsh on Sainsbury, a better cricketer than I would ever be, but he was 41.

The fact was that Peter knew no other life but cricket. A year or so later, he did retire but only to become coach at Hampshire, a role that he did not fill terribly inspiringly, in my view. He had spent his whole career looking after Number 1 and resisting any claims on his place in the team by younger players and now he was supposed to encourage those same players that he had been shunning for years. Old habits die hard. It was difficult for him, as it was for others and continues to be so today, to let go. What next? It looms large in the mind, and it is not a comfortable thought. Some manage to adapt to life after cricket (and I count myself as one of that lucky number), some find it hard and some just cannot cope, with tragic consequences.

For it is an undeniable fact that, together with farmers and dentists, cricketers as a group – admittedly *per capita* a small one – share an unwelcome tendency towards suicide. For farmers, the reasons are self-evident. Apart from eking out a precarious existence, they readily have to hand the means by which they can end their lives, a gun for example. The high rate of suicide among dentists is not so easy to pin down, though spending an entire working life peering into other people's mouths cannot make for a wholly agreeable daily activity. So why should cricketers, who spend their days in a healthy, outdoor pursuit, be so vulnerable to life's slings and arrows? It is a question that has exercised my mind for many years now. Two contemporaries of mine, David Bairstow and Peter Roebuck, died by their own hands and both tragedies lay heavily on the memories of those who played with and against them. Why, why, why, we all asked ourselves. According to the excellent book by David Frith, *By His Own Hand*, published in 1991, 80 first-class cricketers have committed suicide (updated in a later edition in 2001 to 151). That is a shocking statistic. And behind every statistic is a tragic human story.

I have a theory – no more than a gut feeling, in truth – that adaptation to Civvy Street is particularly hard for ex-cricketers. Life up until the cricket bag is packed away for the last time follows an entirely predictable and structured routine, depending on whether you are playing at home or away. The start of play is always 11am, not a minute earlier or a minute later. Lunch is always at 1pm and lasts 40 minutes, not a minute longer or a minute shorter. Tea is of 20 minutes duration, not a minute longer or a minute shorter and stumps are drawn at 6pm. The hours of play have varied over the years and may differ depending on the competition being played but the defined parameters are laid down in black and white.

Cricket is a long game played over one, two, three, four or five days. The schedule is relentless; there are few days off and precious little time for relaxation. The season lasts all summer, and winter too if you are playing abroad. Thus, your team-mates, in whose company you live continuously, become your surrogate family; indeed, you probably sleep with your room-mate more nights than you do with your wife. You share with your team-mates the highs and lows, the triumphs and disasters, of a long and arduous campaign, forging a comradeship that any band of brothers in a war zone would recognise and identify with. Then, when retirement, injury or the sack looms, the dislocation is abrupt, brutal and hard to take. The sensible ones, those with an ounce of foresight, will have planned for this moment. Sadly, many have not and they are left rudderless.

The nature of the game provides additional and peculiar pressures on the psyche. All professional sportsmen and women have to perform; it goes with the territory. A striker might miss an open goal, but he can still score the winner in the 90th minute. A fly-half might drop the ball with the try line at his mercy, but he can still put over a last-minute penalty to win the match. A tennis player can double fault on match point, but he can still serve an ace to win the match two points later. On the final hole, a golfer can miss the fairway but still play an extravagant rescue shot to within inches of the hole and walk off with the Claret Jug. But a batsman makes one mistake, and he spends the rest of the day in the dressing room watching others pile on the runs. It's a long time for moping before there's any chance to make amends. And if he doesn't, and makes another fatal mistake, the time to brood stretches out even further. It's a *foony* old game all right but Boycott might have added that it is a cruel one too, unusually and catastrophically so. It is said that cricketers must be fatalistic about the precariousness of their lot, seeing how fate and bad luck can be so capricious. That is undoubtedly true for the majority, but I am sure there are those who are not so resilient, whatever they may say in public.

The thing is that in professional sport, you cannot afford, under any circumstances, to show weakness. Once the bowler sees fear in your eyes, you are a walking wicket. Once a batsman senses he has the upper hand when you are bowling … well, you won't be bowling for long. And once you have dropped a catch or mis-fielded, it is extraordinary how the ball seems to follow you around. It's a tough and unyielding environment and inner fears and punctured morale are not welcome in a team environment.

The world of a professional cricketer is circumscribed. It may not be a comfortable existence – indeed it should not be – but it affords a life that embraces certain assurances. For a period of time, no matter how short it may be, it is *your* life, one that you would choose over all others. And then, for one reason or another, it is snatched away from you. No wonder the readjustment to another existence is so problematic. I've heard some psychologists referring to it as something akin to a bereavement. I can fully understand that. To me, that sounds like a wholly feasible analogy.

My own experience was quite different (or so I thought). I was stationed at deep square-leg. Quite why I was there I have no idea; it certainly wasn't my usual patch. For those not familiar with the arcane terminology of the game of cricket, let's just say the captain had stationed me at 'cow corner', where the ball usually goes when a batsman loses patience and has a wild slog. I was redundant standing there. Any fool could see that the batsman on strike was blessed with limitless patience. He had been batting all afternoon and was boring everyone to death with his forward defensive and his occasional nudges and nurdles for scampered singles. The only rush of blood he ever had was in his highchair when he threw his rusk overboard. No, the ball was unlikely to come anywhere near me that over.

So, I took a step back over the boundary. For no other reason than sudden impulse. Technically, I was no longer in play. At once, I was no longer a participant in the game but a spectator. I just wanted to know what it felt like. For, very shortly, I was to forsake the life of a professional cricketer and become a bystander. It felt strange. Lines – white lines, red lines, yellow lines, blue lines – assume an importance in our lives far beyond the colour of the paint. Drag his back foot outside the straight line of his crease and that batsman over there could be stumped and put us all out of our misery. Cross a double white line in your car and you've committed a traffic offence. Park on a yellow one and you're in trouble with a warden. Step beyond a blue one and an immigration official will bark at you. And as for a line in the sand … unions have gone on strike and countries have gone to war for less. That white line marking the boundary represented a huge reshaping of my life. Inside the boundary was the snug, familiar world of county cricket, the only one I had known for the best part of the past ten years. Beyond that boundary was the rest of my life. And I cannot pretend that I wasn't suddenly sad and not a little fearful.

I felt detached and a long way from the action. It was all a bit surreal. From this standpoint, in my introspective mood, the game of cricket all of a sudden took on a ridiculous aspect. Imagine that you were a passing Martian, hovering overhead in your spacecraft, enjoying the view, whilst on your intergalactic journey to some distant solar system. What on Mars are they doing, you might ask, all those earthlings dressed in white, standing around like statues in a field. And what's that little, red, spherical object that they're passing around so reverentially? Is it a precious relic or something? Oh, come on, green chaps, let's go. I've had more fun counting asteroids.

I knew this was the end. The cricket committee had not officially informed me that my services would no longer be required. But I knew it was coming so I had saved them the trouble and told them not to bother. The expressions of regret and the good wishes for the future were no doubt genuine – I think I was a reasonably popular member of the playing staff – but I was not a part of their plans for the future and no one attempted to dissuade me from my course of action. This was my last game for Hampshire, and it felt very strange.

I was hardly going out with a bang. Some players end their careers in a blaze of glory, walking through a guard of honour, with everyone on his feet, cheering to the echo the departing hero. Some prefer a less ostentatious send-off and are perfectly happy with some polite applause, a few regretful handshakes and a pint or two in the bar. Others quit the stage with bitterness and rancour in their heart, cutting their ties completely and forever, never letting their shadow darken the place again. A few refuse to take it seriously. A team-mate of mine, John Rice, came off the pitch for the last time, sat down immediately inside the pavilion gate, unstrapped his pads and together with his gloves and bat, he stuffed the lot into a rubbish bin nearby, announcing to all and sundry, 'Well, that's my lot. Goodbye, everyone.'

My farewell could not have been more low-key. It was a home match, but it wasn't at home. That is, it wasn't at the County Ground in Southampton but at one of the out grounds. Some of these places in the rural backwoods of the game were pleasantly attractive – Bath, Cheltenham, Bournemouth, Arundel, Tunbridge Wells, Harrogate, Scarborough, to name a few – but Andover wasn't one of them. Furthermore, it wasn't a first-class match but one in the Second XI Championship. There wasn't a soul there. That was why my bizarre act of stepping outside the playing area had gone unnoticed. The nearest person not dressed in whites was a hundred yards away.

And that was the trouble. The days when I had been excited to play for Hampshire second XI had long since gone. The teams in this competition were made up of either those who were on their way up or those who were on their way down. It had become apparent to me that I had been nudged into the second category; younger players were being promoted ahead of me and it was patently obvious that it was time to go. None of us enjoys the moment of truth, the inescapable admission that we have failed to realise our childhood dream and that our ambition in life has come to naught. Perhaps I was being a bit hard on myself here. My cricket career had not been one of continual disappointment, I'd had my successes, my moments in the sun, and truthfully, I wouldn't have changed a thing. Perhaps with a little more determination, self-belief, good fortune … But life is full of ifs and buts. It's just that I didn't particularly want to stop now. I was edging 30 but plenty of players continued to enjoy a successful career well into their thirties, even forties. Just look at Cowdrey, D'Oliveira, Graveney, Close, Titmus, Gooch. And there was our own evergreen Peter Sainsbury still thriving in the first team when he was 42.

I shook my head to rid it of such self-deluding notions. It was time to give myself a stiff talking to. They were still playing at that age, Andrew, because they could still cut the mustard. They were better players than you. They had more talent. And that was the long and the short of it. You made the best of your limited abilities. Isn't that good enough for you? And, in so doing, you were lucky enough to rub shoulders with some of the greats of the game. Now – get on with the rest of your life.

Ooops, that's over. I should move. But where to? No one is waving at me or shouting instructions. Perhaps they've forgotten about me. I think I'll just stay here. As everyone had changed ends, I was now stationed at deep point, an even more redundant position than deep square-leg. What is the captain thinking about? Perhaps he isn't thinking at all. That happens to even the best of us sometimes. In that case you have to rely on the awareness and attentiveness of your team-mates. I should have run in-field and asked him what the devil was going on, but I didn't. It wasn't a decision born out of disaffection or spite; it was simply the fact that I was quite enjoying these moments of quiet and peaceful contemplation down here. I could even hear the birdsong and the rustling of the leaves as a slight breeze disturbed the trees behind me.

This was very unlike me, I had to admit. Normally, I liked to be in the thick of things, flinging myself around in the covers, active and engaged, close enough to hear all the exchanges, both friendly and acerbic, with the occasional contribution from me. None of that was audible from here. I guess spectators, so far away, are totally oblivious to the chat and the banter that goes on between the players. Maybe they believe that matches are conducted in funereal silence. Nothing could be further from the truth.

I resumed my musing. I was determined not to leave Hampshire a resentful and disillusioned man. I had enjoyed my time and the club had been good to me. And unlike so many others on the scrapheap, I had a job to go to, something completely different, a clear change of direction. It was my father, I suppose, whom I had to thank for this. Once he understood that my intention to become a professional cricketer was a serious one, he accepted the inevitable and gave his blessing, for all his initial misgivings. But it came with a proviso. I had to complete my education first and that meant getting a degree. Which I had done, and I could genuinely put after my name, BA (Hons), English. And so it came to pass that I was to become a teacher of English.

Another stroke-less over. The contest is dying on its feet. Any change in the field? It seems not. This game might be meandering towards a dull draw, but it was the game, the game of cricket, which had secured me the job. Of course it had. Advancement in life has always been largely dependent on contacts and I am sheepish enough to admit that my appointment was no different. The master in charge of cricket at Malvern College, Alan Duff, wished to hand over the reins to an appropriate successor and had contacted a friend who had been an opponent down the years. His name was Barry Reed. Now retired, Reed had been Roy Marshall's opening partner for Hampshire. I knew him well. He was still involved on the coaching side of the club and he it was who had instilled in me a love of fielding, having been a very good one himself. He would have been furious with me had he witnessed my present lack of professionalism towards my fielding duties. Just as well he hadn't; he might have regretted his recommendation of me, as he obviously had done, to Malvern College.

I had been a very naïve interviewee when I went up to Malvern (having had to consult a map to determine where exactly in England it was) and was blissfully unaware of the good words that had been put in on my behalf by several influential people. Thank goodness I had worn a tie. This was by no means an automatic practice of mine; we are talking about the informal 1970s here. And I hated ties. I had been one of the ringleaders in boycotting a tie at a club reception, which had not gone down too well with the committee. As for the long, blonde hair and the bandit moustache, I am not at all sure what the school thought. But at least my manners are impeccable. For that, I have my parents to thank. In any event, I got the job, to teach English and to run the cricket. I shall never forget the look of bemusement on the face of Alan Carter, the head of English, when he asked me what literature I had recently been studying and I replied, after some thought,

The Daily Telegraph. Apparently, when the relevant powers that be were discussing my possible appointment with the head, Alan said to everyone, 'Well, if someone has got to have him, it may as well be me.' Alan Carter, my first head of department, now sadly passed away … I have much to be grateful to him for, not the least of which was his willingness to take a punt on an inexperienced English teacher.

Hello! The most boring batsman in the world has hit one in my direction. Swiftly, I stepped back on to the field of play, sprinted in, gathered the ball and winged it in an inch or two above the stumps. The wicketkeeper didn't even have to move his hands. Perfect. Mind you, I would have been disappointed had it not been. I took pride in my fielding and was good at it. I received the customary, if prescribed, round of applause from my team-mates. 'Now you're up here, Murt,' said the captain, 'you might as well stay. Bit pointless having you out there.' Good thinking, skip. They'll make a captain of you yet.

And they did. Four years later, Nick Pocock was appointed captain of Hampshire. And by then, I had perforce extended my literary swotting beyond *The Daily Telegraph*.

For the next 30 years or so, I immersed myself in the life of a master at a boarding school, teaching English, running the cricket and becoming a housemaster. It was a narrow world but comfortable, familiar, enjoyable and in my more reflective moments, I considered it a not unworthy occupation. If you feel you are making a difference in your pupils' lives that provides job satisfaction, something I have always regarded as worth more than pecuniary reward. 'If you want to make money,' my father always said (a teacher himself), 'don't go into teaching.' He was right.

Even Aristotle, the tutor of Alexander the Great, moaned about the pay.

Mine was a contented existence, challenging but rewarding. In a boarding school, far from the fleshpots of any metropolis, it was necessarily a circumscribed life. I quickly lost touch with cricket – the professional game, that is; as Master i/c Cricket at the College, I was of course heavily involved, though I kept in touch with a few old mates and regularly attended the ex-Hampshire players' annual reunions. Oddly, none of us took the slightest interest at these occasions in what was happening to the current crop of players who were performing out there on the middle. We had more pressing matters to concern us … *How was so-and-so getting on? He's had a bad time of it lately, I hear. I was saddened to hear of so-and-so's death. Still, he had a good innings. Do you remember when he …?* Parochial and inconsequential, no doubt, but symptomatic of the belonging that bound us all.

Slowly, inexorably, retirement from teaching crept up on me. The circumstances of my finishing with English textbooks were far from ideal, as shall be explained in a later chapter, but the question facing me was the same for anybody who finishes a lifetime of gainful employment … what next?

A dear friend of mine then sat me down and read me my fortune. 'I *never* want to hear you say you are retired,' he said. 'You are not. You are setting out on your third career.' He meant writing – which has always been my *profession manque* – but *third?* Oh yes, I had forgotten cricket.

'Sir, I don't know what to write about.' That was the frequent grumble of my students when set a piece of descriptive writing as a task. Write about what you know, I would tell them. Don't write about inter-galactic warfare.

If you live on a farm, write about the animals. If you live in a city abroad, describe that. If your father is a professor at Oxford (one or two were), write about a household full of books. If your father is a scientist, write about what he is researching. 'Sir – I can't do that. My dad is working on a top-secret new weapon.' If your mother has a high-up job in marketing … and so on. Some still wrote about inter-galactic warfare however, seldom very well.

'Writer, write of what thou know'st!' Using this analogy as sound counsel, I started to write, using my twin passions – the English language and cricket – as guiding lights. Thus far I have had seven biographies of cricketers published and I count myself fortunate. Many authors never succeed in getting anything into print. I found former players, some of them the very best in their eras, only too glad to open up and reminisce about their greatest triumphs and their disasters too. It helped that I am a former cricketer, therefore having no need of explanation as to what is a googly or what it is like to travel up and down England's motorways for six months of the year. I attempted to tell their stories sympathetically and interestingly and have thoroughly enjoyed the experience.

The further these interviews proceeded, the more often a current talking point took hold. Increasing numbers of current and former professional cricketers were publicly voicing their troubles with mental health. In our day, nobody would have admitted in a hundred years in the dressing room that he was struggling. That was a sign of weakness and in this environment, that was tantamount to signing your own P45 form. Nowadays, it is very different, it seems, and so much the better.

All of which brings me round full circle. I return to my original question, or questions. Is cricket the problem?

Is there something about the game, the combination of luck and unpredictability, that drives people over the edge? Or is it just that top-level cricketers are necessarily so self-obsessed (no other team game demands personal performance so relentlessly) that they are more prone to depression and mental illness? If so, why should cricketers be more willing to stand up and go public when footballers, rugby players, tennis players, golfers, athletes *et al* prefer to keep a low profile? In one sense, it does not really matter. Each individual battling his demons 'presents' (to use the medical term) differently. No one story is the same. Yet it cannot be coincidence alone that cricketers have been front and centre in the public debate about mental health. The answer to that I was anxious to discover.

As an example of how social mores have changed over the generations, let me take, for argument's sake, homosexuality. As a sexual preference, it has of course been a part of life since the first human societies were formed. With one or two exceptions, successive civilisations have frowned upon the practice, more often than not condemning it as unnatural and sinful. When I was growing up it was still a criminal offence and was only removed from the Statute Book in 1967. No longer a crime but certainly not something to which anybody owned up, in public at least. But now, nobody turns a hair. Same-sex relationships are no longer the object of derision or disapproval. I think our generation can be proud of that shift in attitude. 'I don't mind what they get up to in private,' opined my aged aunt, 'so long as they don't frighten the horses.' Today, our concern for the well-being of horses is no longer anything to do with homosexuality but more to do with the height of the jumps at Aintree.

On the subject of mental health, however, our generation has nothing to be proud of. We took our lead from our parents, I guess, who endured a world war and had no choice but to 'keep buggering on', as Churchill memorably put it. In the Hampshire dressing room of the 1970s if anyone had brought up the subject of mental health the rest of the team would have looked at him as if he was mad. Perhaps one or two of us really were but never had the confidence to admit it. I feel ashamed, looking back, that we were so insensitive to the finer sensibilities of others, but I am sure none of us meant harm. We were just ignorant. Bloodletting as a medical treatment for a variety of ailments – in order to maintain the balance of the 'humours' in the body – was common practice from antiquity until the end of the 18th century. Far from curing the patient, the procedure probably did more harm than good. Yet none of those doctors was motivated by anything other than good intentions. They knew no better. All I can say is that we knew no better. Cricket was a wonderful game, and we were playing for fun – and getting paid for it! The sun always shone, and life was good. Except for some, it wasn't.

Here is a troubling statistic. English cricketers are almost twice as likely to commit suicide as the average male in this country and have a higher suicide rate than in other sports. Overseas, the percentage is even higher. Alarm bells have been ringing for some time and at last, thank God, we are beginning to listen. David Frith in his book, *By His Own Hand*, brought to the public's awareness the shocking number of cricketers who have brought about their own destruction. The desperately sad and poignant fact is that Frith asked former Somerset cricketer and noted journalist and commentator, Peter Roebuck, to write the foreword. In 2011, Roebuck hurled himself from an upstairs window of a Newlands hotel in Cape Town, a shock to all his friends and colleagues but not altogether a surprise. Something had clearly been amiss for some time. In talking about his book, Frith made this comment that has struck a chord and resonated with me ever since. 'The nature of cricket is such that it tears at the nerves.'

Slowly, one by one, former elite cricketers have come forward to admit that their nerves were torn to shreds. Marcus Trescothick was the first to stick his head above the parapet. Initially, the reason given for his flying home during the tour of India of 2006 was that he was suffering from a 'stress-related illness'. I immediately sat up and took notice. That sounded very much like depression to me, a suspicion that was confirmed when he was forced to abandon the Ashes series in Australia later the same year. Sure enough, he announced his retirement from all international cricket in 2008. The public reaction to his troubles was generally sympathetic, a response reinforced by the publication of his book, *Coming Back to Me*, in 2009, in which he bravely and mercilessly laid bare his lifelong battle with unhappiness. He said that the diagnosis of depression and anxiety that was made in his early 30s was as if a fog in his mind had been lifted. Now he knew what the matter with him was – he had not been imagining it during all these years – and was able to take steps to cope. He remains, like me, a 'recovering depressive' if I can put it like that.

Jonathan Trott abandoned a later Ashes tour of 2014/15 after the first Test, citing once again the catch-all ailment of a 'stress-related illness', but this time nobody was fooled. Here was a man as tough as teak whose presence at the crease was probably the most reassuring sight for Englishmen since Graham Gooch, who now believed he was no longer fit for purpose as an England cricketer. Nobody, least of all his team-mates, really believed that and apart from a singularly crass comment from the perennial bad boy of Australian cricket, David Warner – he said that Trott was 'weak' and 'scared' – the public reaction, as it was with Trescothick, was compassionate and supportive. International sport, especially cricket, is exceptionally tough, seemed to be the general perspective, and it can take a fearsome toll on our heroes. Trott was typically forthright about his problems. 'Coming back from Australia, we said I had a 'stress-related illness' and to me that didn't seem good enough. It was a bit grey. But the reason for that was that we weren't sure exactly what was going on.' Five months later, with a proper diagnosis of depression and anxiety, he was sure what was going on. With professional help, he has been able to sort himself out and now, in a much better frame of mind, he is adamant that cricketers who suffer like he did must seek medical advice and guidance.

It was not just Englishmen who were suffering. All right, Jonathan Trott speaks with the clipped vowels of a South African, but he wore the three lions and a crown on his sweater. A couple of years ago, the Indian captain, Virat Kohli, was asked in a press conference how he felt about the news that the Australian cricketer, Glenn Maxwell, had made a decision to take a break from cricket to attend to his mental health. Kohli's response surprised many. 'I'm all for it,' he said. 'I've gone through a phase in my career when I felt it was like the end of the world.' I can remember that 'phase' very well. It was India's tour of this country in 2014 in which he couldn't buy a run. In ten innings, he didn't manage a single fifty. I actually felt sorry for him. It is always distressing to witness a great performer brought low. Tom Graveney explained to me the circumstances surrounding the attempt by the former leviathan of English cricket, Wally

Hammond, to make a comeback playing for Gloucestershire in 1951, having retired from the game in 1947. 'He should never have come back,' Graveney said. 'It was painful to watch.' Incidentally, Hammond, a sad figure, a loner with few friends, moody, private and uncommunicative, fits exactly the description of a depressive.

The point about Kohli was that he was no *ingénue* on this tour, learning the ropes of Test match cricket. He was already a superstar, idolised in his own country and greatly respected abroad. But not in England, it appeared. He knew that the mantle of greatness could never be bestowed on him until he had mastered English conditions. The pressure he put himself under, and the huge expectations placed on his shoulders, must indeed have been intolerable. He had a miserable time, alone in his hotel room with nobody to turn to, nobody to help. Aarkash Chopra, a former Indian Test player and now a commentator, publicly admitted that there was 'no way you could tell your captain or your coach that you're feeling down because you'd get dropped'. Subsequently, several Indian players have broken their silence about mental health issues. It will be the same in other cricket-playing countries. Depression is no respecter of creed, colour, class or country. Latterly, other former players (Andrew Flintoff, Steve Harmison, Matt Prior, Tim Ambrose and Chris Lewis, amongst many others) have come clean with details of their struggles.

By the way, Kohli answered every doubting Thomas who questioned his ability – if there were truly any, apart from himself – in the best way possible. On India's next tour of England in 2018 he out-scored every other Indian batsman, amassing 593 runs in five Tests at an average of 59.30. He no longer felt like it was the end of the world, though the hero-worship of his Indian public remained as intense as ever.

The next high-profile former cricketer who added to the swelling chorus of mental health issues was the Lancashire batsman Graeme Fowler. He is probably best remembered for his immense innings of 201, spread over nine hours, for England against India at Madras in 1985, the first double century by an Englishman in India. This was at a time when 16 English players had been banned for three years having undertaken a rebel tour of South Africa. When the bans expired, Fowler was cast aside by the English selectors after one further Test. His form deserted him and during a difficult season the following summer he found himself relegated to the second XI. He did make a comeback for Lancashire but in 1992, in the middle of a wholesale clear-out by the club, Lancashire dispensed with his services. According to his team-mates, he was one of the most happy-go-lucky fellows you could wish to meet. Ian Botham said of him, 'He made a dressing room tick.' Yet behind this ebullient exterior, a deeply unhappy and self-doubting personality lurked. He elected to open up about his inner turmoil in his book *Fox On the Run* (his nickname is 'Foxy'), an honest and fascinating insight into the daily life of a professional cricketer and his feelings of helplessness when it seemed his whole world was crashing down around his ears. He makes a very valid point that cricketers do lots of physical training but how much is done to prepare mentally for the game? After all, as the *eminence grise* of the airways, Geoffrey Boycott, never tires of pointing out, 'creekit' is mostly played in the mind, rather like a game of chess on grass.

If there are three cricketers who have written books about their battle with depression, there must be countless more who have not, for one reason or another, spoken publicly about their struggles. What we have seen can only be the tip of the iceberg. Mental health is now taken seriously in the first-class game (as is racism – but that is another story) and I know much more in the way of help and support is available through a variety of organisations. The Professional Cricketers' Association, no more than a fledgling trade union when I was playing, has over the years grown in importance and influence and has been at the forefront of supporting both current and former players. Mental health is very visible in its operations. Just a casual glance at its website will provide avenues to a variety of support mechanisms: mind matters tutorials; confidential helplines; wellbeing support; dedicated apps. And to think the nearest we had to any counselling was crying into our beer with a sympathetic team-mate … just as long as he was not a direct rival for a place in the county side.

Today, even in the cut-throat world of professional cricket, it is all right not to feel all right, to borrow the phrase from one of my psychiatrists. Or, to echo that famous strap line, uttered by Bob Hoskins, advertising BT in the mid-1990s: *'It's good to talk.'* So successful was the catchphrase that it has been adopted by the British Association of Counsellors and Psychotherapists. Clearly, talking therapy is beneficial. No longer is there any need, any reason, to suffer in silence.

My task, as I see it, is to persuade these anguished souls to open up about the affliction of depression. It is nothing to be ashamed of, to admit to despair. As I was repeatedly told during my long battle with the complaint, 'You are just as ill as somebody with cancer or heart disease. The only difference is that your malaise is hidden. Nobody can see you hobbling around on crutches or sporting a vivid scar across your chest. But you need help just as much, possibly more, as any patient.' If nothing else, talking about it might persuade others to follow suit. At the very least, it might shed light on the particular strains and stresses that this maddening game that we so love places on its practitioners.

Chapter 1

A Personal Story

FOR 25 YEARS or so, I had been leading an unremarkable but satisfying existence as a master at Malvern College.

Then something happened.

It came as a bolt out of a clear, blue sky. It did not creep up on me, nudging me with increasing urgency so that I could no longer ignore it. One day I was fine; the next day I evidently was not. Now that it has become a regular visitor, so to speak, I often compare it to a tidal wave or a tsunami, one that shortly will knock me over, spinning me head over heels in the maelstrom, such that I do not know which is upwards to the surface and air, and which is downwards to unconsciousness and drowning. But perhaps the simile does not stand up to scrutiny. A tsunami is caused by an earthquake many hundreds of miles offshore. Those in its path speak of a terrible and prolonged shuddering in the ground, a sudden change in the character of the ocean, a distant roaring like the sound of a passing goods train and a noticeable and unusual receding of the tide. Even the wildlife, birds and animals have disappeared; they can sense something strange is in the air. In the first instance, I had no such warnings. Nobody came on the radio to tell me that the forecast for the following day was not so good.

In fact, I had my back turned, waving to the family on the beach, when the enormous wave hit me from behind, knocking the wind out of me, very nearly my life.

The 'it' that I refer to is chronic, clinical depression. Chronic because it is recurring. More than half of patients 'relapse' within one year of treatment. Clinical because it seeks to make a distinction between the layman's understanding of being depressed – in other words, sad, disheartened, fed up – with the medical definition that encapsulates longer-lasting and deep-rooted feelings of hopelessness, desolation and despair, frequently associated with suicidal thoughts and tendencies. Put like that, it sounds profoundly alarming and indeed it is. Did I ever feel like that? Yes, I'm afraid I did.

What caused it? That is a question I am frequently asked, and the simple answer is I don't know. It has been doing my head in (not the most felicitous phrase under the circumstances) trying to figure out a reason. Sometimes a cause *can* be attributed: a life-changing event; trauma; bereavement; divorce; redundancy; illness; financial woe. In short, pretty well anything that results in stress and unhappiness, *'the slings and arrows of outrageous fortune'*, as Hamlet put it. By the way, I truly believe Hamlet is a case study in depression. His father has died (murdered) and his mother has taken as her husband's replacement Hamlet's uncle (who turns out to be the murderer) in what is described as an *'o'er hasty marriage'*. Then Hamlet's girlfriend, Ophelia, drowns herself. Who can blame the poor young man for questioning the very purpose of his existence? But I can claim no such personal disaster and private angst. To me, the misery had no discernible origin.

What's it like in the loony bin? To be fair, not everybody put it like that but if they did, I didn't mind. People with mental problems are not devoid of a sense of humour, an ironic view of the absurdity of their situation. In answer, I can only respond that it isn't too bad. I was incarcerated for lengthy periods of time in three institutions, in Birmingham, in Bristol and in Bromsgrove. So far, I have not reached 'C' in the alphabet. On two occasions, I reluctantly agreed to being admitted; on the third I most definitely did not. 'It is for your own safety,' I was told, 'It's for the best.' Hmm … I was never convinced. It was unfortunate that this enforced stay coincided with the Covid lockdown. So instead of being encouraged to come out of my room to socialise with other inmates, staff and visitors, I was banged up in isolation, in a single room, all my possessions confiscated, with a guard at the door, just in case I felt the need to explore. I was allowed no visitors – not even my wife – and anyone entering the room – medical staff, cleaners, dinner ladies – was dressed in the full hazmat (short for 'hazardous materials' – I never knew that) as if I had Ebola or was a refugee from Chernobyl. Of course, at the height of the pandemic, I sort of understood the reason for the restrictive measures but at the same time I failed to see how being held in isolation was going to help my mood. It made for a lot of introspection and self-analysis, not all of it comfortable. The food …? Reasonable. But then I lived in a school boarding house for 20 years.

One thing you can be sure of during any hospital stay is that you will meet people worse off than you. When I was recovering from my first knee operation way back in the day before the invention of anaesthetics, the chap in the bed opposite me, with whom I had got on famously, died of a heart attack in the middle of the night. His replacement was clearly very ill. He lasted two nights. When Occupant No. 3 arrived, his neighbour alongside leant across and told him, 'If I were you, mate, I'd ask to change beds.' What on earth I, an orthopaedic patient, was doing in a medical ward, I never did discover. But the incongruous fact in a mental institution is that, on the surface at any rate, nobody looks ill. There are no patients with tubes protruding from their body, or shambling figures wheeling respirators around with them, or plastered legs hauled up on a pulley, or ghostly figures with the light in their eyes slowly dimming. But scratch below the surface and you find poor souls who are deeply troubled and severely disturbed. It put my problems into perspective. Or it should have done if only I were thinking straight, which of course I wasn't. Incidentally, it always brought a wry smile to my face whenever I was escorted along a corridor leading to the Mental Health Unit. Clearly, if I was heading in that direction, 'health' was a bit of a misnomer. Similarly, anybody turning left for the Sexual Health Clinic was rather giving the game away as well.

What treatment was I prescribed? Psychiatry and the treatment of mental illness is a relatively young discipline in the history of medicine. As far as full understanding of the brain and developments of 'cures' for its ills, we are still very much at base camp of the ascent. The current school of thought seems to be that no one size fits all, that the enemy needs to be attacked on several different fronts. On the understanding that my disorder might have at its source a chemical imbalance in the brain, I was put on a regime of heavy-duty drugs. This had the effect of dulling the pain, but it also deadened my sensibility. According to my wife, I was like a zombie, lifeless behind the eyes. Perhaps it acted as a sort of holding pattern, but it clearly could not remain as a long-term strategy. The consultant who put me on these drugs that smashed through the ceiling of 'recommended dosage' later admitted it was her last throw of the dice. Successive consultants who have read her notes have told me that she was very pessimistic of my chances of … how can I put this … of not, at some stage, taking my own life. Quite possibly, her decisive intervention saved me.

The cavalry, the spearhead of the offensive, to extend the military metaphor, is Electro-Convulsive Therapy (ECT). It sends an electrical current through the brain causing a brief surge of electrical activity, a seizure in other words. It sounds brutal and bizarre, rather like the brainchild (ha ha!) of somebody who has strayed from the pages of Mary Shelley's novel *Frankenstein*, but it has been medically proven to alleviate some mental health problems. There were long and detailed discussions with me, most of which I could scarcely remember, before I gave my consent. Quite frankly, by that stage I hardly cared what happened to me. I might as well give it a go was my reasoning; nothing else seems to be working. Accordingly, I underwent two separate courses of six interventions each.

The process, as opposed to the actual procedure, was simple and painless enough. We patients gathered in the waiting room. Some I recognised from my unit; others were from nearby hospitals. All were grimly silent. There was no conversational exchange, no commonplace observation, no attempt at banter to relieve the tension. Each no doubt had his or her inner demons to battle. When you are called, you cannot help but notice the spaghetti junction of electrodes and wires lying beside your head as you lie down on the bed. We've all no doubt been 'put under' with anaesthetic before an operation. This was no different. The next thing I remembered was the distant voice of a nurse welcoming me back to the here and now with a cup of tea. I felt no ill effects and so long as I put out of my mind what was actually happening to me when unconscious, it didn't seem so bad. Possible side-effects are occasional gaps in memory but as I can't remember them, no great harm seems to have been done. But were there any beneficial effects to this treatment? Once again, it is hard to tell. I'm still here so I cannot categorically claim it was totally ineffective.

The groundwork of the assault is provided by the poor bloody infantry, the talking therapists. Actually, it would be more accurate to call them listening therapists for any such treatment should always be 'patient-led', to use the jargon. Talking about myself has never been my strongest suit. In fact, growing up, our generation was discouraged from displaying such self-absorption. 'But that's your problem,' I was continually told. 'You bottle everything up.' Quite possibly, but I found those sessions excruciating when you all sit in a circle, introduce yourself and tell everybody – at great length – what a grand chap you are and how the rest of the world doesn't appreciate you. But in the hands of one or two sympathetic and perceptive therapists, who teased out possible personal crises in one-to-one sessions, I felt I was making some progress.

So, am I better? Better, yes, but not best. I have concluded that the condition can only be managed, rather like diabetes or alcoholism, on a day-by-day basis. Which interventions have worked, and which haven't? I would love to know the answer but Sherlock Holmes's *modus operandi* 'When you have eliminated all which is impossible, then whatever remains, however improbable, must be the truth' cannot, in all practicality, be applied in my case. If one part of my medication were withdrawn, and subsequently all of it, I might be fine. But I might not. It is an empirical experiment that is just not worth the candle. So, I am stuck with that unhelpful parrot perched on my shoulder offering ugly and unpleasant advice. I know he's there. I just have to take him on and outmanoeuvre him in the metaphysical debate ... *every single day.* I can't pretend it's not a struggle. The only alternative is oblivion and truthfully there are times when oblivion seems like an attractive option.

I retired from teaching a year before my 60th birthday. Malvern College were good to me and looked after me with all due care and support in order to clear the decks and to train all my guns on the enemy. It did not take me long to appreciate that mental health is the Aunt Sally of the NHS: under-funded, under-resourced, under-manned. In all, I came under the care of five consultant psychiatrists. As one after another retired or moved to another part of the country I began to worry that I was driving them away, but the truth was that all of them were feeling the strain with inadequate support in place and the meagre support they did have was being stretched to breaking point. Much as I sympathised with, and understood, the logistical problems they were facing, I felt I was dropping off the radar. Who had their eye on my deteriorating state?

Quite ironically, it was Anno Domini that came to my rescue.

'Hang on a minute,' said my charming South African GP, 'I see you're 70. I had no idea. I thought you were years younger!'

I did say he had charm. He also loved cricket and we would spend most of my consultation time with him chatting about the game.

'So what?' I asked.

'That means you are eligible for mental health support in the community for ... ahem, the elderly.'

Oh, wonderful. I had to reach my dotage before anybody took any notice.

Recognising this was ungrateful, I thanked him and shortly became a regular visitor to a mental health unit conveniently situated in Malvern. Thereafter, I was in the hands of two impossibly young women, whom I came to trust and who challenged me in ways that I hitherto thought were impossible. Those of my generation were not supposed to contemplate our feelings, our thoughts, our self-awareness. If anything was wrong, or if we suffered some form of personal catastrophe ... well, come on, stiff upper lip and all that. Worse things happen at sea.

Methodically, diligently but kindly, these two intrepid ladies set about deconstructing what I had held to be fortitude of mind, a grin-and-bear-it attitude to life. Nothing was off-limits, no avenue was left unexplored, no memory left buried. Parents, Catholicism, childhood, schooldays, adolescence, university, professional cricket, public school, fitness, diet, family ... it was all laid bare. I cannot pretend that I did not find these searching examinations deeply uncomfortable but for the most part, I think I held it together. Willy-nilly, we are all products of our upbringing, our domestic and social background and there was a lot – more than I ever imagined – to get off my chest.

Yet I did not have an unhappy childhood. But I was unhappy. I was at a loss – still am, frankly – how to explain this anomaly. My wife, looking at all the team photos of me in cricket and football teams at school, remarked that, even though I was always sitting as captain in the middle of the front row, I looked like a haunted little boy. I say 'little' because I was, always the smallest and most frail. My nickname was Murt the Squirt. It was only when I entered the sixth form that I started to grow.

The problem, we decided, was that I suffered from an acute lack of self-confidence. This might come as a surprise to anybody who knows me, but I have developed over the years an ability to don a cloak of poise and equanimity. I was a teacher after all, and teachers are actors. They love an audience; they have a different one eight times a day. Looking back, I have to say that I did not enjoy school, not until the sixth form years. This had nothing to do with the teachers or the institution I attended; it had to do with one glaring, unavoidable, burdensome and actually quite harrowing hole in my intelligence. One subject loomed grimly every day of my school life. I dreaded the period and wished the ground would open up and swallow me as the lesson commenced. My mind, for some reason, was closed to figures and sums. Put simply, I was innumerate. But in those days, such an affliction, much like dyslexia, did not exist. It was just an excuse for laziness, an unwillingness or inability to *learn*.

* * *

Let me go back a little. My father was a good man, albeit a little intimidating. Three sturdy pillars supported his world – education, family and Catholicism – and I am not at all sure that they were necessarily in that order. He came from a staunch Catholic family, counting two priests and one nun among his siblings. He was a headmaster and clearly his children's education was important to him. And family? Perhaps it would be more accurate to call it duty towards his family. He was a man of firm principles and believed in a life of self-sacrifice and discipline, robustly but fairly administered. He fought the Japanese in the jungles of Burma during the war. I often wondered what terrible things he must have witnessed but by the time I was brave enough to ask, it was too late. Like many of his generation, he never talked about his experiences. He put them in a drawer and locked them away. Do I detect a pattern here?

The only school in town, as far as he was concerned, was the Catholic grammar school, run by the order of De La Salle Brothers. In order to gain a scholarship (with five children, and on a teacher's salary, he could not afford the fees), I had to pass the Eleven Plus. This comprised three papers: English, Arithmetic, General Intelligence. English was a doddle and GI was not difficult, but Arithmetic was a closed book. My father would fire questions on the times table at me during mealtimes and he would become increasingly exasperated at my panicked and of course wildly inaccurate answers. It was clear to him, and to me, that the Arithmetic paper would be my undoing. As it happened, I passed the Eleven Plus, though I have no doubt that strings within the Church were pulled. I entered St Joseph's College, Beulah Hill, in south London, with a scholarship.

My travails with Maths did not end there, however. It was a given that I should go to university. After all, my older brother, something of an academic *wunderkind*, had gained a scholarship to Oxford and the same was expected of me. (My younger brother was 'as bright as a button' as well as my father kept on telling me, which didn't help my self-esteem.) Of course, I knew that O Level Maths was a prerequisite of entry into any university back then. But the more I tried to unravel the mysteries of numbers – I possessed a slide rule, as we all did in those days before calculators, and the only use I could put it to was to scratch my back – the more I felt as if I was beating my head against a brick wall. In any end-of-term exam I took in the subject the highest mark I ever obtained was 5%, and all I could do was wonder where the 5% had come from.

To my father's frustration and pain, I took Maths O Level three times and failed with a worse mark on each occasion. As it happened, I did manage, somehow, to find the only university on the planet (Southampton) that did not require Maths O Level to read English. My uneasy relationship with numbers has remained with me ever since, though calculating declarations (number of overs against the total required – run rate in other words) has never been a problem. It's guesswork largely, though guesswork informed by experience and gut feeling.

I don't blame my father. He was motivated solely with my best interests at heart. Perhaps his methods would not find approval nowadays, but he was only trying to keep me out of the local secondary mod, where I would undoubtedly have sunk. Incidentally, he mellowed in old age and became the most gentle and loving grandfather you can imagine. I still wish I had plucked up the courage to ask him about his wartime experiences. He seemed moody and distressed by many things when we were younger. Quite possibly, he too suffered from depression. From what I have read about the Burma campaign, it would hardly be a surprise.

Has all this baggage from my childhood come back to bite me later in life? Are childish terrors revisiting me? It all sounded a bit Freudian to me, but I was content to accept that all this *might* have contributed to my disorder. To combat these feelings of worthlessness, I have to remind myself continually – as I have been taught to do – that my life has not been a failure. Indeed, there are those who might think that there have been one or two successes along the way.

Another line of enquiry – and if that sounds like a piece of police procedural, that is exactly how it felt – was my relationship with sport, in particular the playing of games. 'Look at all the injuries you have had,' I was told. My response was that I had only ever had one injury, though its recurrence at various stages of my life was certainly adding up. A torn cartilage when I was 20 put paid to my football career and that was certainly a huge blow. My father, a talented amateur footballer in his time, believed I was a better footballer than cricketer but as he was an Irishman who never played cricket, I would have to take that with a pinch of salt. But I knew I was a good player; just how good I would never have the chance to find out. Further injuries and subsequent operations on the same knee finally stopped me playing cricket.

My professional days were over by that stage, but I still wanted to play at a decent club level. The competitive juices had not dried up, however. I turned myself into a half-decent squash player. I had the goal of becoming a double county player – at cricket and squash – and slowly I climbed the Worcestershire rankings. When I reached No. 8 or 9 in the pecking order, I felt I was within touching distance of the county team. Unfortunately, there are only five players in a team, so I knew I still had work to do. Then the old knee (I say old because now I have a new one) finally gave way and that was that. Now I play a bit of tennis and am grateful that I can do so, enjoying the game without taking it too seriously.

But this is familiar to all games players, I told my therapists. Injuries and a slow disintegration of the body go with the territory.

What's so special about my tussles with getting old? Ah, just because it is common, I was told, does not mean that it is insignificant. For each individual, the uncomfortable truth has to be faced and many ex-sportsmen and women struggle when the reality hits home. Once they were strong and fit and took joyous delight in their physicality, the elation of possessing a body at the peak of its powers; now they are a shambling wreck, with every bone creaking and aching, a pale shadow of their former selves. I was amused at the description of my possessing a body at the peak of its powers, but I accepted there was some truth in the analysis. 'Each time you had to give up what you loved doing was like a little death,' they said. An intellectual can grow in knowledge and reason as he gets older; a games player slowly loses what first defined him.

'Age I do abhor thee;
Youth I do adore thee.'

William Shakespeare

Chapter 2

The Mind

'The mind is its own place, and in itself
Can make a Heaven of Hell and a
Hell of Heaven.'

John Milton, *Paradise Lost*

I READ a book not so long ago which attempted to explain the origins of life. Apparently, an infinite number of coincidences, accidental occurrences and miracles in effect coalesced to form a galaxy and an infinite number of coincidences, accidental occurrences and miracles coalesced to form our solar system. Furthermore, another extraordinary set of coincidences came together to make our planet, Earth, capable of sustaining life. The journey from the earliest known life form, microscopic organisms (microbes) to *Homo sapiens* is equally characterised by an infinite number of forks in the road. If a single wrong turning had been taken at any time on this tortuous journey, I would not be here at my desk typing away at my computer.

The question I ask myself is not how we came to be here – I can leave that to the scientists – but *why*. That conundrum has exercised the minds of philosophers, theologians, scholars, psychologists, academics and thinkers down the millennia. If it took an infinite number of miracles to bring us to where we are, must there have been a superior being watching over us, making sure that we always took the correct fork in the road at every step of the way? But why make it so long drawn out and so perilous? In many ways, the story that God made the world in seven days – well six, actually, because He was so knackered after this burst of creative activity that He had to lie down for a rest on the seventh – is easier to grasp, no doubt the reason that the theory had so much traction for so long. Or is there no such thing as a guiding light? We have all been hoodwinked by religion – it's just chance.

These existential musings prompt a further question. What is it that separates us from other animals? Why are we what we are? Hamlet spends five acts pondering this very mystery. In the end, he dies none the wiser. Nothing has been resolved in his mind, nothing achieved. He doesn't know what to believe, what is truth and what is false. All has been a waste of time. There is no universal answer. Man, he concludes, is nothing more than '*a quintessence of dust*'. His final words are, '*The rest is silence.*' Not much spiritual succour there. I'm not Hamlet but I do wonder why we humans are capable of introspection when other animals are not. My dog doesn't spend hours contemplating the meaning of life; all she worries about is where the next meal is coming from.

I am intrigued, as a result, with the brain, that grey, squishy mass of fat and protein about the size of a grapefruit and shaped like a walnut, that sits atop our neck and shoulders. It allows us to think and communicate through language, giving us a highly developed intellect that is capable of reasoning, feeling and self-awareness, all of which separates us from beasts. I have suffered from clinical depression, eliciting, whether I have liked it or not, a more objective contemplation of the mind and what can go wrong. The study of the chemical and electrical impulses that the brain interprets does not really interest me; that is a technical and scientific corridor down which I could never journey, even if I had the most patient teacher explaining it all. No, my interest lies more in why the mind plays nasty tricks on us, not how.

At first, I was confused by the distinction between 'psychology' and 'psychiatry'. Psychology is the study of the mind and its functions, especially affecting behaviour. Psychiatry is the study and treatment of emotional disturbance and abnormal behaviour. Good. I'm glad that is clear to everybody because it isn't to me, even now. Which definition applied to me, I wanted to know. The answer is that probably the two disciplines, the two areas of expertise, bleed into each other at the edges. Was I being treated by a psychologist or a psychiatrist? I never really did find out.

Trying to make sense of the mind is nothing new. There is a historical line of philosophical thought going as far back as the Ancient Greeks (Socrates, Plato, Aristotle, Epicurus, Archimedes) to the Romans (Cicero, Seneca, Plutarch) through the Elizabethan and Renaissance periods (Erasmus, Copernicus, Galileo, Bacon) to the Enlightenment (Kant, Rousseau, Voltaire, Descartes, Franklin *et al*) and that's not including the Chinese and Indian traditions. But it was not until the 19th century that meaningful, science-based research into experimental psychology started up in earnest. The science in succeeding years has grown exponentially to the extent that you might be forgiven for thinking that the field has become a bit crowded.

The current methods to help people such as me when their minds stray off-piste are varied and flexible. In the old days, the village idiot was tolerated in the community, even cared for. By the 18th century lunatic asylums had started to spring up to house the insane. The most famous in England was the Bethlem Hospital (from which we get the word 'bedlam'). The 19th century saw a shift in attitudes to mental illness towards a more compassionate treatment and, by the 20th century, more radical physical therapies were being developed with new theories promulgated, new interventions practised, and new drugs tested. Today the emphasis is much more on talking therapy, mindfulness, counselling, cognitive behaviour therapy (CBT), all delivered alongside, sometimes instead of, a drug regime. No one size fits all, it seems. The enemy must be attacked on many fronts.

So where does all this leave me? What have I gained from the whole process that has surrounded, sometimes overwhelmed, me? What have I learned about the mind and its caprices? The answer to that is equivocal – a great deal and not much at all. How can this be? That sounds very much like an oxymoron. Let me try to explain. The more I think, the less I know. Or perhaps I should say, the more I learn, the greater the illimitable vista of ignorance stretches out in front of me. Consider those maps of Africa in the 16th and 17th centuries. The coastline of the continent had been discovered and mapped but the interior had not yet been geographically explored. It was left largely blank. That is my concept of the brain. Much has been revealed but there are still enormous gaps in knowledge and understanding.

In the end, nobody knows, nobody can possibly know, what goes on in another person's mind. Very often, a person doesn't even know what is going on in his or her mind, let alone somebody else's. Our thoughts are our own, to be shared guardedly, by degrees, piecemeal, often self-serving with a watchful eye on our ego, our soul, our essential being. In Arthur Miller's play, *The Crucible*, John Proctor rips up his false confession (to witchcraft), telling the court he cannot lie to save his skin. Asked why he will not sign and save himself from the hangman's noose, he cries out, '*Because it is my name! I cannot have another in my life.*' In other words, nobody, not even the state, has the right to peer into an individual's mind. In an effort to bring to an end religious intolerance and the burning of heretics that had characterised the reigns of her brother, Edward VI and her sister, Mary I ('Bloody Mary'), Elizabeth I declared, '*I have no desire to make windows into men's souls.*' Both she and Proctor understood the essential privacy of the mind. All we can do is develop the awareness of our own feelings and practise recognising those of others, at the same time understanding that we are usually guessing. Educated guesses, one hopes.

Like Hamlet, I marvel at the infinite capacity of the human brain. '*What a piece of work is man. How noble in reason. How infinite in faculties … In action, how like an angel. In apprehension, how like a god.*' But like Hamlet too, I understand – and accept – that my mind will die, cease to exist, become no more than the skull of Yorick, the old court jester, that he discovered in the grave being dug for Ophelia. '*Alas, poor Yorick. I knew him, Horatio: a fellow of infinite jest, of most excellent fancy.*' Look at him now, Hamlet continues, the bile in his gorge rising at the very sight. What he is pointing out, in effect, is that the human spirit, the mind, the brain, is capable of great things but that it is mortal, just like the rest of us.

Would we want to go back to the earliest origins of man, to the Neanderthals, presumably content in their ignorance? After all, they knew no better. They never had to worry about depression and '*the heartache, the thousand natural shocks that flesh is heir to*'. But that's a futile thought. We are where we are, to use a hackneyed phrase. You can't uninvent the wheel, the internal combustion engine, the motor car. Here's another analogy that springs to mind. Our spanking, brand-new Alfa Romeo, equipped with all the latest bells and whistles, breaks down. While we wait by the kerbside for the AA to arrive, an old man in a horse and cart trots past. There is a lot less that can go wrong with a sturdy horse and a well-built cart, but it won't get us home very fast. Perhaps that is the price we have to pay for a highly developed brain; occasionally, it can blow a gasket.

My interest is not wholly driven by scientific or psychiatric curiosity but more particularly to understand why a gasket seems to blow more frequently in a cricketer's brain. Graeme Fowler in his book posed the rhetorical question: cricketers spend much time training the body but is any thought given to training the mind? I pose a further question: is it *possible* to train the mind? In a broad sense, of course, the brain is being trained at every thinking moment of our lives. What Fowler means, I believe, is can the emotions be harnessed in order for the elite sportsman to perform at his best? Some do it automatically. They have the ability to 'switch off', to empty their head of noise and to concentrate exclusively on what needs to be done. Others find this difficult. They are subject to 'nerves', they are easily distracted, they lose concentration and do not give of their best. Most cricketers, I would imagine, fall somewhere in between these two extremes or, more likely, find they can concentrate fully on one day but not the next. This is the problem that coaches and sports psychologists have to wrestle with in a team environment – how best to prepare their charges to do battle out there, in the middle.

The brain is split into two hemispheres. Our thoughts continuously flit from one to the other as different parts are accessed. Anxiety lies on one side, calmness on the other. The ideal state for any competitive sportsman or woman is at a balance of the two extremes. Too anxious and optimum performance is impaired; too laid-back and the game is lost.

Fear of failure, 'performance anxiety', as it is called, or 'nerves', as it used to be known, does not permit the player to relax and think logically. Focus is required to perform well. I remember talking to the former West Indian opener and Hampshire captain Roy Marshall. He was a fearless batsman who believed in attack in an era when the opener's job was traditionally seen to blunt the fast bowlers, not put them to the sword. 'You look so calm out there,' I said, 'as if you were playing beach cricket back home in Barbados.' He chuckled ruefully. 'I'm as nervous as a kitten before going out to bat,' he admitted to my surprise, 'but once I step on to the outfield, the butterflies disappear. All I can think of is hitting the ball.' Often and very far, I can add.

Some cricketers are paralysed by fear and never do their huge talent justice. Others with less talent seem able to rise to the occasion. The harder the task and more challenging the circumstances, the better they play. It's what we used to call 'having a good temperament'. The best batsmen have learnt how to select their goal – scoring a hundred – but have the ability to break down into sequential steps – every ten runs, say – the journey to the desired three figures. They block out all outside 'noise' like sledging, for example, or excited chatter, excessive appealing or the shouts of the crowd in order to pay attention to what is required in their innings without over-analysing. Bowlers, too, need to select their goal – getting this batsman out – but they must not lose the plot in their desperation to take a wicket. They have plans and strategies to put into effect. They need to think exactly where they want to pitch the ball and concentrate on that and that alone. As they run up, they must put to one side all the helpful and sometimes unhelpful advice from their team-mates and the roar of encouragement from the crowd. They must focus exclusively on the bit of turf, no more than a square foot, where the next delivery must land.

Can this skill – concentration without obsession – be taught? I'm not so sure, despite the assertions of sports psychologists that it can. I believe that it can be *practised*, how best to control emotions on the field of play, but seminars, tape recordings, self-help books and crib sheets ... ? Perhaps. Just because we had no access to such aids when we were playing does not mean that we should throw the baby out with the bathwater. If more attention is paid to the mental wellbeing of our cricketers, spotting the early signs of mental distress, as eloquently chronicled by Trescothick and Trott, and nipping them in the bud, then so much the better.

Stillness of mind, perfect concentration when body and brain are working in perfect harmony, was a state I attained all too infrequently in my cricket career, but I do know what it feels like and was in awe of those who seemed to manage it on a regular basis. Too often, thoughts of inadequacy and fear of failure would crowd in, so rudely that I would almost wish not to be there. There is a smidgen of reassurance in understanding that I was not alone; indeed, far better players than me have owned up to similar feelings of anxiety. Hoping for the best but expecting the worst; that was my trouble.

Not the sort of trouble that would beset the best batsman in the world. I refer to Richards. That is, Barry Richards, not Viv Richards, though none who played against King Viv would ever deny his claim to greatness. As a former team-mate of Barry's, I am naturally biased, but the mantle of genius was bestowed on him by just about any of his contemporaries I have ever spoken to. I witnessed many of his great innings first-hand, but one exhibition stands out in my memory. It was in the nets. Some clown had thoughtlessly deposited one of my medium-paced deliveries into the long grass at the far end of the ground. I trudged off to fetch it. I had noticed Andy Roberts standing around, bored and uninterested seemingly. He was in fact *lurking*. As soon as he saw Barry padding up, he grabbed a ball from the box and marked out his run. The game was afoot! Here was the fastest bowler in the world bowling to the greatest batsman in the world. Everything went quiet. The rest of the Hampshire team continued to bat and bowl but everybody's attention was focussed on the duel about to unfold. So engrossed were they, including the captain and coach, that nobody noticed, or did not care, that I had not returned to my bowling duties but had taken up a position immediately behind Barry, a front row seat of the drama, praying that the net would hold firm against Andy's thunderbolts.

The next 20 minutes was the most riveting passage of play I have ever witnessed – at a net practice! Barry for once eschewed his natural flamboyance and grandstanding at net practice (he once turned his bat round so that he played the ball with the edge and challenged us to get him out – we never did) and concentrated on playing properly. To do otherwise with Roberts bowling would have invited serious injury. Besides, ego, pride, bragging rights were at stake. Neither would take a backward step. Reputation was on the line.

Who won? I guess the answer to that is a score draw. Barry did not smash Andy to all parts. But neither did he get out. In the end, they both called it a day and repaired to the dressing room for a restorative cup of tea. But I had been fascinated by how Barry coped with balls being bowled at him not far short of 100mph. I instinctively flinched whenever he let one go as it thudded into the back net a mere few inches away from my face. What struck me most was how much time he seemed to have to play the ball. He was never rushed or flustered or beaten or even hit. It was a masterclass in playing fast bowling of the highest class.

Apparently, a batsman has 0.44 of a second to react from the moment the ball is released at that pace to the moment he must hit it or choose not to hit it. It is actually physically impossible to track the ball at that speed, judge where it is going to bounce and decide which shot to play. In that case, how could Barry have played Andy so comfortably? How could anyone ever score a run when there is, in point of fact, not enough time to react?

I rely on scientific research for the answer. There is too much for the brain to compute, to judge what the ball will do in the air, where it will pitch, what it will do off the pitch and then decide what shot to play, in that half-second. So, Barry, seemingly with time, had in fact no time. What he was doing was intelligent guesswork. His brain over years of playing the game had learnt the physics of a moving ball, even at great pace, and then he was moving into a rehearsed motor movement to meet the ball. We call this 'technique'. For all his extravagant strokeplay when the mood took him, Barry possessed a classically orthodox technique. 'Learn the rules first,' he used to say, 'before you can break them.' His boyhood had been spent in the nets under the careful and critical eye of a school coach who taught 'according to the MCC coaching manual', as we used to say. I am not at all sure what Barry would have said if I had told him that his batsmanship was based on 'intelligent guesswork', but I understand the concept of a batsman playing a shot without thinking. I once had the privilege of opening the batting with him against Leicestershire. I was being peppered by bouncers from Graham McKenzie and Ken Higgs. 'They don't do it to you,' I complained between overs. 'Because the last one they bowled to me, the ball was last seen bouncing down the M1,' he smirked. All I can say is that he was obviously a better guesser than me.

Incidentally, good eyesight has nothing to do with it. It was only after he had retired that Barry owned up to the fact that his eyesight had been deteriorating for some time. During World Series Cricket, he had been experimenting – unsuccessfully, as it turned out – with contact lenses. He still ended up with a higher average in the Super Tests than anybody else, above even Viv Richards, Greg Chappell, Gordon Greenidge, Zaheer Abbas *et al.* Famously, when Donald Bradman had his eyes tested, it was discovered that his eyesight was 'below average'.

Although a bowler does not have to react (not in the same way, though he does of course have to adjust his tactics when a batsman hits him for six) he does have to clear his mind and have a mental image as he runs up of exactly where he wants to pitch the ball. He too moves into a well-rehearsed motor movement as soon as he starts his run. This will include his approach to the crease, where he lands his front foot, how he is gripping the ball, what he does with his wrists and fingers as he lets go and where and how he follows through. This is a physical action that has been repeated thousands of times and should, by now, come naturally. Yet, sometimes, this repeatable action breaks down. It's known in the business as the 'yips' and when it happens, usually for inexplicable reasons, the results can be uncomfortable to observe, even for the most hard-bitten professional.

It happened to two former team-mates of mine, both fast-medium bowlers. One relied on bounce and movement off the wicket; the other was a swing bowler. Both lost rhythm and then confidence and the struggle for them even to land the ball anywhere near the business part of the pitch was painful to watch. Both were forced to give up the game, their skill seemingly having deserted them for good. Another excruciating occasion when an attack of the yips left the poor bowler in tears happened to a good friend of mine and a subject of one of my books. The incident was laid bare in his unflinching description, which, incidentally, he was anxious to be included in the text. John Holder, Barbadian born, was making a name for himself at Hampshire as a more-than-promising fast bowler. By 1970, he reckoned he was bowling as fast as anybody and seemingly had the world at his feet. He directed me to the scorecard of the Hampshire v Kent match that season at the United Services Ground in Portsmouth. Kent's total was 310. John Shepherd scored 105 and Mike Denness 64. The next-highest score was extras with 40. Unusually high. 'I bowled 12 wides and 19 no-balls,' said John. 'I just didn't know what was happening to me. I was running in, and I just didn't know where it was going. My control of the ball completely deserted me. In the end I was walking back to my mark, head down, feeling unbelievably low, the crowd were jeering, and I just wanted the ground to open up and swallow me.' In a situation like that, even the batsman feels sorry for the afflicted and makes no effort to take advantage to score a few cheap runs.

In the same era, Fred Swarbrook, a respectable slow left-armer for Derbyshire, inexplicably 'lost it', overnight. His bowling more resembled a baseball pitcher, with full tosses and head-high beamers. One ball went in the air vertically and landed on his head. He tried everything, including seeing a psychologist who suggested putting a pebble in his pocket which he was instructed to rub for luck before each delivery. Nothing worked and he soon faded from the game. Ravi Shastri, the Indian cricketer, suffered from the yips. As did Phil Edmonds. He completely lost his run-up, something that most people would find hard to believe, seeing as a spinner's run-up consists of not more than a few paces. In the end, Edmonds dispensed with any sort of run-up at all; he would lurch forward and deliver the ball. Remarkably, his actual bowling did not suffer. And who can forget poor Simon Kerrigan's torment at the Oval in 2013 during the final Test against Australia? He suffered a catastrophic attack of the yips and in the end was barely capable of landing the ball on the cut strip. Yet apparently, he had been bowling superbly in the nets just before the game.

There was no physical reason for these difficulties, no shoulder injury, for example, that would have affected their action. Why should a repeated motion that has been performed countless times suddenly and inexplicably break down? It is not just a cliche; cricket really is played in the mind.

Traditionally and historically, the incorporeal essence of a living being has been the immortal soul, in Ancient Greek known as the 'psyche'. If you look up 'soul' on Wikipedia you will find pages and pages, practically an encyclopaedia, of philosophical thinking on the subject. Cicero, the Roman statesman and polymath, once said, 'A room without books is like a body without a soul,' which neatly encapsulates how important the concept of the soul was in the ancient world. In subsequent civilisations, the heart was regarded as the symbolic home of the soul, the body's nerve centre of all emotion, as Aristotle argued, which is quite a heavy burden for an organ that is essentially just a big muscle. Thomas Carlyle, the great Scottish philosopher and man of letters of the 19th century, wrote that 'a loving heart is the beginning of all knowledge'. Not that the heart was the repository of exclusively loving sentiments. It could harbour evil just as readily. 'Vengeance is in my heart!' cried Titus Andronicus in the eponymous play by Shakespeare.

Modern science informs us differently. We now know that the brain is the key to our existence, the seat of all our thoughts, emotions and feelings. We still use the word 'heart' and 'soul' poetically, as metaphors for something we feel, deeply and viscerally, as in, for example, 'he put his heart and soul into this project'. But the brain is the command-and-control centre of everything we do, say and think.

If we are in a good mood, we are more likely to seek new experiences, be creative, plan ahead, adapt, make sense of the world. If we are in a 'good place', we are more likely to perform at our best. Feeling buoyant, confident, alert but relaxed, is usually the prerequisite of a fine innings or a good spell of bowling. Few cricketers who have lain awake all night consumed with anxiety or who have already mentally envisaged failure tear up trees. The confident do not allow misstep or possible defeat to intrude into their consciousness, or if they do they immediately banish such thoughts from their mind. By contrast, people with depression find it very difficult to function at all, let alone perform at their best. They brood, they ruminate, they 'catastrophise' (another buzz word of psychotherapy that I have learnt; people who catastrophise always believe the worst is going to happen). In this state, the sufferer has poor concentration, sluggish energy levels and sees the world through a cracked prism. His thinking has become buckled, awry, off-centre. He is stuck in a vicious circle, a vortex of bleakness and self-loathing. A part of the brain truly is misfiring. Not a recipe for a breezy innings or a wicket-taking burst.

In his famous Ashes series of 1981, when England overturned odds of 500-1 when facing certain defeat at Headingley, Ian Botham, helmetless, with his team at 137/7 in the second innings, 92 behind and facing an innings defeat, decided it was time for him to cut loose. He scored 149 not out and inspired England to a victory that has entered cricket folklore. Earlier in the series, Botham had been sacked as captain. The removal of responsibility and obligation seemed to energise him. He said later that he had gone out to bat without a care in the world and simply thrown his bat at the ball, even laughing as attempted hooks flew off the top edge over the slips. There was a man not suffering from self-doubt; his thinking was entirely positive. He looked and probably was happy in what he was doing. I doubt anyone with depression could possibly have played like that.

That is not to say that no thought or tactical flexibility operates in a game of cricket. There was method in Botham's madness. He was attempting to sow the seeds of doubt in the Australians' minds (he certainly did that). It was a counter-offensive, he took the fight to the enemy, he threw everything bar the kitchen sink at them to turn the tide of the battle. He was far too wily and experienced a cricketer to believe he could, or should, always play like that. Indeed, his century in the fifth Test at Old Trafford was, technically, far superior. He believed he had never batted better. 'That innings at Headingley was a slog,' he said. 'The Old Trafford hundred was a *proper* innings.'

Cricket is a complex game. By contrast, football is a simple game (simple but not easy). I often feel that coaches over-complicate football. Basically, when your team has the ball, you run into space. When your team loses the ball, you close down the nearest man. The game is capable of weaving the most intricate, even magical, patterns but it is beyond me why any coach feels the need to produce flip charts to explain what a substitute has to do. The sub is anxious to join the fray. He's jumping up and down to loosen the limbs and dispel the nerves. He is nodding in agreement, but I bet not a word shouted in his ear penetrates his mind. Rugby is a complex game, with a host of laws and set pieces and ways of playing. But that game is over in 80 minutes. There may well be extensive post-mortems later, but they are discussions conducted in reasonable tranquillity. Cricket is a long game and there is often little or no time to reflect and regroup collectively after play or between matches. Players will be scanning their road maps or these days punching postcodes into their sat-navs as they face the prospect of another trip along England's motorways. 'Bad luck, old son – brute of a ball you got there,' will be the single acknowledgement of your private torment as your driver switches on his favourite playlist at full blast. And you are left to ruminate bitterly for the next two or three hours on your latest failure. Yes, professional cricket is a merciless mistress.

The pressure to perform is intense. No more so than any other sport but cricket is unique in that a player's achievement or lack of is laid bare at every step of the way. In a football match, the score is recorded on the board or on the screen, but the number of chances that a striker has spurned is not shown. Nor are the number of missed tackles by each player in a rugby game posted for the whole world to see. But the dreaded 0 against your name is up there on the scoreboard prominently displayed and stays there all day. What's more, it will be in the newspapers the following morning. You hope that the printmakers' union has gone on strike, but they never do in the cricket season. If you have had a 'quiet' game on the football or rugby pitch, there is every chance that the correspondent of the *Daily Rag* will not even mention you. But in cricket, the scorecard never lies. If your name is not mentioned in the match report, the printed scorecard offers you no such anonymity. As you trudge off for lunch, the scorer hares across from the scorebox to present the team with a breakdown of the bowling analyses. If you have had a nightmare of an opening spell, it will be you having the breakdown; every run scored off you is there, writ large in the figures on the page. Nowadays, the increased use of technology means that your deficiencies in technique and execution will be pored over in super-slo-mo by your coaches and even more alarmingly, by those of your opponents. The scrutiny is relentless. Bad performance is well-nigh impossible to hide.

All this stress adds to the fear of failure, an insecurity that cricketers do their best to conceal. You cannot afford to show weakness to the enemy, but neither can you admit to self-doubt to your team-mates. If you do, you feel you are letting everybody down. And underlying this judgement is the feeling that you are letting yourself down. You haven't come up to scratch. You cannot cut the mustard. You are simply not good enough. Is it any wonder, therefore, that those already in a fragile frame of mind begin to feel acutely depressed, especially if the poor form persists and Lady Luck has deserted you?

Cricket is a slow game. Play unfolds at a measured pace and every match has its *longueurs*. There is even time between each ball for the spectator to continue his conversation with his neighbour. Plenty of time for that poor fellow in the slips who has just dropped a sitter to mull over his public embarrassment. The best players, those with a resilient temperament, those who can shrug off misfortune, those who have 'bottle' (some might call it a thick skin, a lack of imagination) are beset by no such mental ambiguity. Ray Illingworth was one such character. According to his team-mates in the Leicestershire dressing room, 'Raymond was never out'. He came back after having been dismissed, complaining bitterly about the blinding reflection off the cars' windscreens in the car park adjacent to the sightscreen. 'But Illy,' piped up one brave soul, 'it's cloudy today.' Amusing of course because Illingworth, either deliberately or unconsciously, was playing up to the archetypal image of the self-righteous Yorkshireman. This unshakeable belief in your own importance and the insignificance of every other individual in the world – well, at least out there on the pitch – may not be an agreeable personal trait but it is unquestionably a useful tool as a cricketer. We could all name players, both in our own team and opponents who never nicked it or who never bowled a bad ball. There was always somebody or something else to blame. Irritating at the time but I do wonder if a bit more of this utter self-confidence would have benefited me. Others too, judging by how much the topic of depression in the game has come under public scrutiny.

Let's face it, cricket is a bloody frustrating game. Luck plays a huge part. Form is like a will-o'-the-wisp, here today, gone tomorrow. And the next day. And the day after that. Then you worry, over-think and start to tinker with your technique, which only seems to make matters worse. As a result, you dread being dropped from the team and ultimately you fear that you will not be offered another contract and that your career will come to a premature end. There is much time spent away from home, without the comfort blanket of sensible advice from your family. It must be worse on tour. There is always somebody in the squad who will benefit from your failure. It can be a very lonely place as you brood, only pretending to be fully on board with exercises in team-bonding, the jokes, the fun and games, the camaraderie.

I have recently finished writing a book on Lord MacLaurin. One of his many roles in public life was chairman of the English and Wales Cricket Board. He was horrified when he took hold of the reins to discover that the England team stayed in inferior hotels to the accompanying England officials. He soon put that right. This immediate upgrade for the team meant that now each player had his own room. Hitherto, players had always shared. An unintended consequence of this largesse and treating England players with respect was that any member of the team who was struggling emotionally could now shut himself away in his room and no one would be any the wiser. Before, his 'roomie' would have sensed that something was wrong, and no doubt offered support and encouragement. If the situation deteriorated, he would seek help and advice from the management in a way that the sufferer would not feel able to do. I am sure, following Trescothick's and Trott's sad public demise, a closer eye is now kept on international players' mental well-being.

Another question I pose in this exploration of the mind of a cricketer: does the game attract those of a more self-analytical disposition? The game is very technical. There are as many styles and methods as there are batsmen. Often you can identify a batsman simply by observing his stance. No two run-ups and actions of bowlers are the same. There are only so many ways you can kick a ball, but cricket lends itself to individuality and as such can provoke endless tinkering, not all of it helpful. At Hampshire, we had a coach called Geoff Keith. In many ways, he was born for the role. He was a theorist, an analyst, a guru of technique. There was nothing more he enjoyed than dismantling your batting, piece by piece, back-lift to follow-through, and then attempting to build it up again. Some of us did not find this helpful. Mark II was often less successful than Mark I. He would spend hours shadow-batting in front of the mirror in the dressing room, even when our innings was taking place. Instead of observing how his charges were getting on out there in the middle, he was checking where his back-lift was going.

Once, when I found myself at the opposite end to him when he was batting, he came up to me between overs. 'How do I look?' he asked. 'As handsome as ever, coach,' I answered. 'No,' he persisted, 'where is my head when I play the ball?' Frivolity was my stock-in-trade when

I was playing, doubtless a smokescreen to cover up my insecurities. I was tempted to reply, 'On your shoulders, coach, where it always is,' but I forbore. He was forever tinkering with his own technique instead of putting some backbone into us younger players. After each ball, he would carefully rehearse the shot he had just played, or should have played, instead of putting it aside and concentrating on the next. Apparently, as a young man, great things as a Hampshire batsman had been predicted but somehow, he had never fulfilled his early promise. The older players at the club said that he over-thought the art of batsmanship and lost sight of the simple, basic purpose of that bat in his hand ... to hit the ball. Sadly, tragically, because he was a lovely man and liked by everyone, he developed a brain tumour and died one winter when we were all abroad playing and coaching.

Geoff may have been an extreme example, but cricket lends itself to fierce self-examination. Which of us at some time in our career has not adjusted his grip, experimented with taking middle, instead of middle-and-leg, guard, lengthened or shortened his run-up, tinkered with his action, crouched at different heights and at different angles in the slips? When all is going well, everything is best left alone. But more often than not, everything is not going well. Sometimes it is going very badly indeed, and something must be done. That is when doubts about technique creep in and little changes made. And if they don't work, alarm and confusion grow – ideal soil for depression. Cricket is that sort of game. There is not the time to brood in other games. There is plenty of time in cricket. Sometimes too much. Apprehension also finds expression in routine, or more specifically, superstition. We are all prone. We could identify the little fads and eccentricities of each member of our dressing room and no doubt he could identify ours. Mine was *always* strapping on my left pad before my right. Unless I was not scoring runs. Then I would swap, for better luck. In the end I didn't know what pad to put on first. It seemed easier not to pad up at all and just give up. Thank heavens I quit the game before I went mad, for that way surely madness lies.

'You must not say or think you are mad,' I was repeatedly told during my psychiatric treatment. 'You are not. You are ill, just as if you had diabetes, cancer or heart disease.' I took a lot of persuading. Sometimes my affliction felt very much as if I was mad. Then my English language training would kick in. The word 'sane' is derived from the Latin word '*sanus*', meaning 'healthy'. The antonym of 'sane' is 'insane'. Thus, the definition of 'insane' must be 'unhealthy', or to put it another way, 'poor health of the mind'. Not really madness at all, just a little twinge, or a pulled muscle, or a passing infection, in the brain, not much different from any other part of the body. In such a way my mind would attempt to make sense of what actually appeared irrational, inexplicable, unknowable.

We have all heard of the Latin phrase '*mens sana in corpora sano*'. A healthy mind in a healthy body. That is what we should all strive for, we believe. Anything that the physical training instructors of the Royal Marines take as their motto ought to be good enough for us … a happy balance between body and mind. Such equilibrium is easy to parrot but difficult to attain.

A friend of mine, who knew I was contemplating writing a book about depression, lent me a book to read, *Back from the Edge*, by Luke Sutton. Apart from noting the rather clunky cricket pun that seems to be the pre-requisite of all cricket autobiographies, I had not heard of the person nor his subject. On starting to read, it soon became clear that the subject matter was relevant to my project and what's more, resonated loudly with me on a personal level. His writing style did not particularly appeal but that wasn't the point. As soon as he mentioned the Priory on page 6, I immediately sat up and took notice. I too have spent weeks in the Priory, on three separate occasions and in three separate locations. There are many such institutions dotted around the country, providing professional care for a variety of acute mental illnesses and to them I probably owe my life. Here was a fellow cricketer (he played variously for Somerset, Derbyshire and Lancashire) who had to retire from the game in 2011 on account of his self-confessed battle with depression. Even on page 1 of his book the description of his state of mind brought all my old terrors flooding back.

'Here I was, sat on my bed, staring out the window, tears pouring down my face, in a place some describe as a "rehabilitation centre" and others, more honestly, call an "acute psychiatric hospital". Where did it start and finish for me to end up here?'

Precisely. How did it end up like this for many of us? In writing this book, that is what I wanted to explore.

Chapter 3
The Priory

'WHERE HAVE you been?' enquired a friend who had not seen me for a while.

'In the Priory,' I answered, a trifle disingenuously.

'I didn't know you had "got" God.'

I hadn't. I still do not 'get' God, in the sense that I am a committed Christian. The Malvern Priory, it should be said, is a church, parts of which date back to the 11th century. Let us not forget that these magnificent Norman cathedrals, abbeys, minsters and priories were originally decorated in the most gorgeous colours, much of which was stripped away during the Reformation, when such artifice was taken as dangerously popish. The Malvern Priory is no exception, the jewel in the crown of one of England's most famous beauty spots.

But, of course, it was not the place of worship to which I was referring. When it was decided (I had little say in the arrangement) that I had to be admitted to a secure psychiatric hospital, the choice, in the first instance, lighted upon Bristol Priory. As my wife drove me up the sweeping drive, through extensive grounds to an attractive Grade II listed old manor house, even in my febrile state of mind, I could not help but think, well, if I have to be banged up in a loony bin this is not the worst place to be. From my childhood, I have memories of a lunatic asylum, as they were called in those days, situated near to where I grew up, in Tooting, south London. That looked a grim and forbidding place; it even had a security wall, topped with menacing rolls of barbed wire. It didn't look a lot different from Wandsworth Prison, not many miles away. This place could not have looked less like a prison, more like a stately home. The reasons for my incarceration have already been outlined in an earlier chapter but here I want to describe the experience as accurately as I can, given that I was in no state to observe critically and dispassionately and my memory necessarily was not as sharp as I would have liked.

* * *

In my interviews and fireside chats with other sufferers who have been good enough to open up about their time in the Priory or similar institutions, I found how remarkably similar were our recollections. First, as we stepped over the threshold, a feeling of panic took hold. I never, at any stage, seriously believed I was *that* bad, but here I was checking into – or rather, being checked into – a psychiatric hospital. I must be worse than I thought. Bewilderment too mingles with a maelstrom of emotions. How on earth did it come to this? I had lost control of my life and that is no easy thought for someone who always prided himself on his self-control, of being in charge, of coping well with life's vicissitudes.

Reception was little different from a hundred hotels into which I had checked during my cricket career. Everybody was friendly and solicitous. It was only after I had bidden farewell to my wife, been escorted down the corridor and shown to my room and there left to unpack, that despair enveloped me. I dropped on to the bed, buried my head in the pillow and wept tears of pain and wretchedness.

I don't cry. Well, of course I do. But not in front of anybody else. Imagine my horror as I heard a muffled voice through the enveloping pillow.

'Hello, Andrew. My name is Muriel. I'm lead nurse on this corridor. I've come to check your belongings, just to make sure that you haven't got anything that might … well, harm you.'

'Like a loaded pistol?'

No, I didn't say that. Humour – even the most mordant type – was a stranger to me at that point. Razors, nail scissors, nail file, tweezers were all confiscated.

'What happens when I want a shave?'

'Just pop along to the nurses' desk at the end of the corridor and ask for one.'

So, what would stop me now from cutting my throat that I would not have been tempted to do at any other time? But it was pointless arguing. One thing I swiftly discovered was that the nurses were relentlessly cheerful but inflexible about the application of the rules. They had no choice, I suppose. Their responsibility for their patients' safety within a volatile atmosphere is enormous. But an objective assessment of the difficult job they perform was beyond me at this stage. All I could feel was anger and a burning resentment at my wife who had abandoned me, the doctors who had taken away my freedom, the nurses who were now keeping me in prison and that bloody silly woman who had confiscated my razors. If only I had stopped to think, if only I had been capable of thinking, I would have realised that my state of mind was truly out of joint.

This befuddlement as to why I was in the Priory finds its echo in the accounts of others I have spoken to or read about. John Barclay, a contemporary of mine in the professional game, has always been aware of what he calls a 'sensitivity of mind' since adolescence. To this day, he knows the enemy is ever-lurking in the shadows, ready to pounce at any moment. For some reason he cannot fathom, it seems to strike at times in his life when, paradoxically, things are going well. In 1981, in his first year as captain of Sussex, he had led them to second place in the County Championship, as surprising as it was gratifying. As he set out for a second stint coaching and playing in Sydney over the following winter months, he not unreasonably considered, and started planning for, a campaign the next season when second would be converted to first. Whilst captaining his club side in Sydney grade cricket, he was aware that he was losing the plot. He was scattering his fielders around the pitch like confetti with no idea how or why they were there. The names of his players escaped him and the orders he was barking out were directed at unknown people. 'Nobody noticed what was going on,' he told me 'Probably an indictment of my captaincy,' he added with a typical touch of Barclay self-deprecating humour. At the club, they may not have noticed anything strange about his behaviour but his wife, Mary-Lou, certainly did. She phoned her mother back in England who advised her to get in touch with a doctor in Sydney, whom she knew. The doctor took one look at Barclay and the next thing he knew he was admitted to a private clinic, by the sea, just out of town. 'It was a low moment,' he recalled.

Luke Sutton, on the other hand, knew perfectly well why he was in the Priory, but it had taken the intervention of friends to book him an appointment. He had not gone willingly, but he had known for some time that his life was spiralling out of control. He was deeply unhappy, lost in a fog of rage and self-loathing, drunk most of the time, and lonely. 'I had so little clarity,' he wrote in his book. 'My brain was cloudy and confused. I was broken. I didn't know anymore who I actually was.'

So, there we were, all three of us, past professional cricketers, at different times in our lives, sitting on a bed in an acute psychiatric hospital, staring blankly out of the window, feeling lost and confused and fearful what the future may hold. To the nurses keeping a watchful eye on us, this would be a normal and expected reaction from newly arrived inmates and was not a state of mind that should be left to fester.

Slowly a regime starts to emerge. As in any institution, mealtimes provide a structure to the day. Sutton remembers walking into the dining hall to be confronted by a sea of strange faces and feeling absolutely terrified. 'It reminded me of my first day at Millfield Prep as a young boy.' Barclay remembers his first breakfast in hospital. 'This was a ghastly meal and hardly designed to prolong the will to live … we queued up at the canteen where all manner of goodies were on offer but very little got eaten. I had a go at the poached eggs, but rarely did I eat them.' My experience was not much different. I always seemed to be sitting on the same table as a painfully thin young girl. She was obviously being treated for anorexia. Her plate of food lay untouched in front of her. Sitting alongside was an enormously fat nurse, whose job, it soon became clear to me, was to ensure that this girl ate her food. The look of stubborn fury on the girl's face suggested that was a forlorn hope. In all the time I was there, I never saw that girl put a single morsel of food in her mouth.

Compare these experiences of mealtimes with those that we would have been familiar with when playing cricket. Food disappears rapidly. Table manners are not of the highest order but to be fair, lunch and tea breaks are short and there is a game to be won. Conversation, often with stuffed mouths, is loud, cheerful and occasionally raucous. Nobody picks unenthusiastically at the plate in front of him. Cricketers are healthy, active animals with large appetites. Evening meals, back at the hotel or at a local restaurant, are lively affairs where the deeds of the day are picked over in detail. Above all, they are social occasions. We were part of a team, enjoying each other's company. The Priory was most definitely nothing like that.

The odd thing about mental institutions is that everybody looks quite normal, apart from that poor anorexic girl. We can all call to mind images of mad houses, lunatic asylums and old mugshots of people clearly deranged. Nobody here was shuffling around with soiled clothing and unkempt hair and the wild look behind the eyes of the severely unhinged. Perhaps they, the certifiable insane, were incarcerated elsewhere. Everybody here looked perfectly sane to me. But something was missing. It took me a while to discover what. Everybody was guarded, secretive, withdrawn, reclusive even, as if each one of us was battling with our own demons, fighting our own private ghosts, unwilling or unable to allow any relief column into our castle. I made no friends there, nor did I want to. Barclay said he made only one friend during his stay, a chap called Dave. In his final group sessions before being released, Dave was asked what his plans were for when he left. 'Get a passport and go to Denmark,' he replied. Why Denmark? 'My wish,' he replied, 'is to live somewhere I can have sex with underage boys.' There was a shocked pause before he added, 'And Denmark seems as good a place as any.' Even in his darkest moments, John

Barclay is capable of appreciating the essential absurdity of the human condition. 'I knew Sydney was the gay capital of the southern hemisphere,' he said, 'but that remark was as surprising as a Viv Richards duck.'

Luke Sutton's experience was different. He made friends easily and the bonds he forged with his colleagues in group therapy were intense. 'You pour your heart out to them,' he wrote, 'and they know more about your life than anyone else in the world.' He was obviously a better patient than me. I would rather have died than pour out the secrets of my heart in front of strangers. Perhaps his suffering was of a different type to mine. He was put on the Addiction Therapy Programme (ATP), on account of his drinking problems. From reading his book, I deduce that alcohol was not the problem, it was only a symptom, an escape, a drug really. The problem was within his soul, his perception of self, his lack of a lodestar in his life. But of course, he had to dry out.

Alcoholics are by nature gregarious people. Drinking is a sociable activity and helps to oil the wheels of human intercourse. The trouble is that the warning sign, the amber light, is run and that's where jeopardy lurks. As the days stretched out in front of me at the Priory, I became aware of a noisy, jolly gathering each evening just outside my bedroom window. They were all smoking, offering each other fags from their packets. Every so often, one of them would get up to go and collect a jug of water from inside. On his return, he would cheerfully but carefully go round topping up everybody's glass. Then it struck me. These were recovering alcoholics. They were trying to recreate as closely as possible, but with glasses of water rather than booze, the camaraderie of a group of people getting noisily and merrily drunk in the pub. I cannot say whether this was so for Luke Sutton, but he seemed to be searching for a way that neither John Barclay nor I were.

Gradually, a routine of sorts started to emerge. Most of it centred around different species of talking therapies, all of which I found excruciating. At first, we would sit in a circle and the lead counsellor would ask us each in turn to introduce ourselves, talk about our lives and what was troubling us. Some dreadfully sad stories would emerge, and my jaw would drop as people began to uncover their shockingly chaotic, even violent, domestic circumstances. How can anybody behave like that? How could anybody do that to another human being? What sort of parenting was that? No wonder my fellow patients are in such a state. These were the horrified reactions racing through my brain as one by one these damaged people told their stories. Some broke down utterly and were consoled by others with tissues, glasses of water and comforting arms around the shoulder.

Did any of this soul-baring encourage me to follow suit? Frankly, no. Apart from my natural aversion to navel-gazing, I did not honestly believe I had a story to tell. I had not been abused as a child, my parents had not divorced acrimoniously when I was young, I had not been bullied at school, my wife had not run off with my best friend, I had not been made redundant, I had not been forced to file for bankruptcy, I had not suffered horrific injuries in a car crash … my life seemed mundane in comparison to some of the tales of woe to which I was being forced to listen. All I knew is that I was trapped in a downward spiral of misery and desolation. And try as I might, I could find no logical, concrete explanation for it. Talking therapy seemed a waste of time. Eventually, I became bored with these sessions and paid no more than lip service to the whole procedure.

Somebody who embraced these sessions with a fervour bordering on zealotry was a Welshman with an ego the size of one of those valleys from where he repeatedly told us he hailed. He was about my age and there was something familiar about his voice. 'Look, I will level with you,' he said, a phrase that was on page 1 of his book of cliches. 'I am a well-known politician ...' Of course! I knew him. He was as much of a windbag in the flesh as he was on radio and television. He talked and talked and talked, mainly about himself, and for the life of me I could never remember at the end of his monologues what point he had set out to make at the start. Just occasionally, I would attempt to interject with what I thought was a witty aside – anything to interrupt the torrent of words – but one thing I learnt from my stays in these hospitals was that humour was in short supply. There was no banter, no repartee, no raillery, no teasing, no levity, no laughter – just impenetrable gloom. I had been used to the wisecracking and badinage of the Hampshire dressing room and the Malvern College common room. They were lively places. In the Priory, everybody was morose and self-absorbed. It may have come as a surprise to some of my fellow patients, but it is still possible for a person with depression to crack a joke.

John Barclay is in agreement with me in his experience of life in a psychiatric clinic. 'Much of the time I was bored,' he said. 'There wasn't much to do and, by and large, few patients felt like any activity.' He too found the group sessions largely unproductive but his admiration for the staff, endlessly patient and doing their best in the face of deep apathy from their charges, knew no bounds. One large, no-nonsense Aussie therapist he admired hugely. 'Jan was fantastic. Her language was a bit rough but if she had been any good at cricket, I would have wanted her in my team.'

Luke Sutton, by contrast, made friends easily in the Priory and took up the group sessions enthusiastically. There was much that he needed to get off his chest. He told stories and recounted incidents of shameful behaviour when drunk; it was almost as if confession, to himself as much as anybody else, was required before expiation. Encouraged by the lead therapists, he saw these sessions very much as team-bonding exercises, a familiar role for him, a county cricketer and a captain as well (of Derbyshire). Once mutual trust had been forged, he knew that the time was right for him to unburden himself. 'We were always encouraged to spend lots of time with our group peers, mealtimes, coffee breaks, evenings, etc. … we helped each other.'

All I remember is long hours, alone in my room. Nobody was helping me. But of course, they were. That nurse permanently sitting outside my propped-open door. It annoyed me at first being under 24-hour surveillance but then I began to feel sorry for him or her. How very boring keeping an eye on somebody lying on his bed, staring at the ceiling, lost in his self-pity. Sutton was on half-hourly checks and felt mightily pleased with himself when the checks were dialled down to one hour.

Both Sutton and Barclay had suffered close emotional bereavement, and I was interested to discover whether the grieving process had had any bearing on their mental problems. My sister, we believe, had died by her own hand but that was over 30 years previously; it was heart-rending, but I had many happy years after that event before I hit the wall. I cannot ascribe any more significance to that family tragedy than it would have been for anybody. Sutton's girlfriend had died in a car crash. He was adamant that the event was not the cause of his problem. 'I didn't end up in the Priory,' he wrote, 'because of Nia dying. There were warning signs and progressions long before I had even met Nia.' Barclay's wife died of cancer. 'Of course, I grieved,' he confided in me, 'and I went through all expected stages of grief. But eventually, I came out at the other end. So, no, I can't really point the finger at her passing as a reason for my depression.'

There were comical moments in the madhouse. Soon after my admittance, I was startled out of my reverie by a strident alarm bell. 'What's up?' I asked of the nurse whose turn it was to be on suicide watch by my door. 'Fire drill?' She shook her head, unconcerned by the commotion. 'Somebody's done a runner,' she announced matter-of-factly.

I came to rather enjoy these regular escapades. A patient would burst from some door or other, thus setting off the alarm. And then the nurses would give chase, across the gardens, in full view of us all. The problem was that the nurses, both male and female, were, almost without exception, overweight and unfit, and the runner usually wasn't. It amazed me, and still does, that so many nurses, or health providers, as they are called these days, are so unhealthy themselves. To see them gathered in groups outside in the garden smoking would made me shake my head in bafflement. Surely they, of all people, who see and care for seriously ill patients, possibly dying, shouldn't smoke. I wondered when the penny would drop. Incidentally, the posse in pursuit of their quarry would return half an hour later, empty-handed, red in the face, sweating furiously, gasping for air. The runaway would later be returned, either by the security on the gate or by the police.

'I escaped a few times,' Barclay announced. 'I just strolled out of the front door and walked the short distance to where we were living.' I was dumbfounded. My friend had never struck me as the Ronnie Biggs type. 'But wiser counsel always prevailed,' he admitted. 'After a cup of tea, I would be driven back and delivered to the front desk, where I was told I would have to serve my time.' Punishment block, Johnny? 'A week's solitary with all privileges removed,' he laughed.

The Priory – of which there are 42 in the country – is a chain of institutions, whose stated aim, their 'mission statement', to use the current terminology, is to provide 'specialist mental health treatment'. The English teacher in me would want to point out that if you're healthy, you wouldn't need treatment but when I was one of their patients, I was hardly in any fit state to cavil over the use of language. But my point is that mental disorder is a broad church. It's as if orthopaedic, surgical, natal, geriatric, renal, neurological, oncological, rheumatology, radiology and all the rest of the disciplines were lumped together in one department. There were people under the same roof as me who were suffering from a wide range of disorders. They were the ones who could be easily identified and categorised: those suffering from depression, obsessive-compulsion disorder, post-traumatic disorder, schizophrenia, anxiety, eating disorders and addictive behaviours, including alcohol and drugs. There were others, I am sure, whose demons were deeply buried and mystifying even to their doctors.

In short, there is not enough staff, equipment, accommodation or money to go round, to care for all those poor souls in need of professional help. The Priory – all of them – do their best to fill the breach and their standard of psychiatric treatment is second to none. But they are private organisations, and their fees are not cheap. BUPA paid for my time in residence. What about the unfortunates who could not afford such specialised treatment? But this is not a political treatise. Mental health has always been the Aunt Sally of the NHS. How to rectify this imbalance occupies far more knowledgeable minds than mine. I ask myself only this; what benefit did the three of us, Luke Sutton, John Barclay and me, gain from the experience?

Sutton believes that the time he spent as an in-patient was life-changing. 'As I left the Priory,' he wrote, 'I knew I had an opportunity to change. But it was down to me.' He had dried out and four weeks later, he announced his retirement from first-class cricket. The road ahead had many potholes and bumps, but he managed to stay sober as he rebuilt his life. He is now an agent for a number of high-profile sports and media stars, looking after other people rather than being obsessed with his own performances. He is, he concludes, an immeasurably better person for the experience.

Barclay puts his recovery down to the good medical attention he received at the hands of his doctor. Though he did not appreciate it at the time, the enforced rest at the clinic was what he needed. 'My doctor had the wisdom to reintroduce me to the drug lithium, which I should have been taking all along, and together with a strange mixture of anti-depressants, I began to get better.' *Lithium?* 'Yes, I know. I always thought that was what they put in batteries. Probably right. My batteries needed recharging.' I had raised my eyebrows at the mention of lithium. I had been prescribed the drug, but I had not got along with it. It gave me the shakes.

'I find I'm okay if I keep taking it, even to this day,' Barclay insisted, and then made another pertinent point about his stay in the clinic. 'This was 1982, don't forget. I was the newly appointed captain of Sussex. Of course, there was no way that I wanted news of my incarceration to leak out. Admitting mental health problems in those days was professional suicide, so I covered it up, and any subsequent episodes, by calling it glandular fever. Yes, glandular fever came to my rescue on several occasions. Now, years later and middle-aged, I find myself asking, 'Why be ashamed of something beyond your control?'

Why indeed? But I too found professional reasons for dissimulating about my enforced absence from school. By then I was a housemaster at Malvern College and my wife concluded, probably correctly, that parents might not be too happy about their son being looked after by a man consigned to a psychiatric hospital. She went to great lengths to hide the real reason and as a consequence, the rumour mill was working furiously. 'Thank God you're back,' said one parent. 'We'd all decided you had AIDS.' By the time I had my third period of hospitalisation, public opinion was shifting, and the stigma of mental ill-health was slowly being dismantled. Like Luke Sutton, I felt my time as a teacher was up and soon afterwards I retired to concentrate on what I am doing now, forging a third career as a writer. Malvern College were very good to me, supporting me with sympathy and generosity of spirit and ensuring that my departure was financially favourable and emotionally painless. I should like to hope that all institutions today are similarly enlightened.

I had mixed feelings about my time in the Priory. At all times, I was well cared for and there is no doubt that the staff's dutiful and constant attention saved me from myself. The therapy sessions I thought were a waste of time, but that was probably my fault. The problem was not the courses or the proficiency of the lead therapists but my emotional reserve. The woman who turned me around was my consultant psychiatrist. She was calm and talked sense. She encouraged me not to beat myself up about being depressed. She convinced me that I was not mad but that my mood most probably, insofar as anybody can be sure about what goes on in the human brain, was on account of a chemical imbalance; the electrical points were misfiring. After much trial and error, a regime of drugs was prescribed ('heavy duty cocktail', my GP son calls it), which seemed to work and still serves me to this day. How long will I be on this Venlafaxine and the rest? She smiled. 'For the foreseeable future.'

Chapter 4

A Case Study

Wally Hammond

'There are two sides, two players. One is light, the other is dark.'

John Locke, English philosopher and physicist

HAD IT not been for Donald Bradman, a convincing case could have been made for Wally Hammond's place as the finest batsman in the world between the wars. Far from taking pleasure at being mentioned in the same breath as Bradman, Hammond deeply resented the comparison. In public, he affected not to take much notice of The Don's record-breaking achievements but deep down, it rankled. 'Not only do I have to do well,' he privately complained, 'but I also have to score more runs than Bradman.'

Before we seek to deconstruct the flawed personality of Hammond, it is as well straightaway to remind ourselves of his record. If a Test batsman averages in the 40s, he is considered to be a very good player. If he averages in the 50s, he is considered to be exceptional. It is only when he averages in the 60s, can he legitimately lay claim to greatness. Only three batsmen in the history of the game thus qualify: Graeme Pollock (60.67), George Headley (60.63), Herbert Sutcliffe (60.63). A fraction below this trio lie: Ken Barrington (58.67), Hammond (58.45), followed by Garry Sobers (57.78). (There are others with averages above 60 – Adam Voges, Barry Richards and Sid Barnes – but it could be argued they played too few Test matches to justify the label of 'greatness'.) By that yardstick alone, Hammond can be counted in the highest echelons. Of course, it does not need me to remind you that Bradman's average was 99.94 (it would have been over 100 if he had scored 4 instead of a duck in his final innings), a figure so far in advance of others that commentators have argued that his record is the greatest achievement of any sportsman in any game. That is what Hammond felt he was up against every time he went out to bat for England. Another point worth making is that Sobers also took 235 wickets, which allows him undisputed claim to the greatest all-rounder who ever lived. I mention this because Hammond was a bowler too, a reluctant one, admittedly, which would account for his relatively meagre count of 83 Test wickets, but contemporaries said he could have been a genuine Test match all-rounder, if only he had bothered. Incidentally, he was a slip fielder *par excellence.*

But as ever with bald numbers and statistics, Hammond's Test match average only tells half the story. In the same way that Denis Compton would empty the bars when he came out to bat (Ben Stokes would be today's equivalent of 'box office' appeal), it was the majesty of Hammond's strokeplay rather than the number of runs he scored that took hold of the imagination. Take the two Englishmen ahead of him in the averages, Herbert Sutcliffe and Ken Barrington. Both were run-gatherers, neat, compact and unfussy accumulators, batsmen that would grind an attack into the dust rather than put it to the sword. Hammond was in a different class. Known primarily for the power and beauty of his driving, he could, of course, when push came to shove, play shots all around the wicket – he would hardly have survived, let alone flourished, at Test level had he not been able to do so – but it is the cover drive that was his signature shot. There is that famous photo of him playing it at Sydney in 1928; one look at it and you can understand why the eye was instinctively drawn to him whilst at the crease.

'Of lovely, athletic build, light as a ballet dancer on his feet, he was the outstanding batsman between the wars. His game was based on driving, and nobody was his peer when it came to the cover drive.'

No, not a description taken from the pages of *Wisden*, nor a portrait from the pen of that doyen of cricket writers, Neville Cardus, but from the lips of the very man who *was* indisputably the outstanding batsman between the wars … none other than Hammond's nemesis, Don Bradman. Oh, that Hammond could have shown equal generosity of spirit. Team-mates of his at Gloucestershire, when news of yet another record set by Bradman filtered through to the dressing room, could hear Hammond muttering under his breath, 'Fucking Bradman!'

For Hammond was, for all his extravagant gifts, not a very nice man. Accounts of his peevish temperament, his arrogance, his moody and uncommunicative spirit, his selfishness, snobbishness and unfriendliness, abound. He was unpopular amongst his peers; some of his team-mates came to hate him. It is true that Bradman was not always popular in the dressing room, but he was respected and admired. Hammond was roundly detested by many who knew him. Even his most loyal friends, of which there was a handful, eventually fell out with him.

Historians regard primary sources in their research as gold dust. First-hand accounts, eye-witness reports, contemporaneous written chronicles supersede any amount of re-written narratives, unreliable sources and faulty memories. I had the good fortune to have a story about Hammond told to me by one who was actually in a dressing room with Hammond. George Chesterton, the subject of my first biography, was one of those schoolmaster-cricketers who would put away their books at the end of the summer term and turn out for their counties for the rest of the season. Not all of them were worthy of their place but in those days, if an amateur expressed a keen desire to play for his county, more often than not, he would replace a professional in the side, who probably relied on the match fee to make ends meet, in a way that the well-off amateur did not. But Chesterton was worth his place in the side; in fact, Worcestershire desperately needed him. 'Never mind, lads,' the captain, Peter Richardson, would console his players after another defeat. 'Cheer up. George will be with us next week.' After finally retiring from county cricket, Chesterton continued to play for MCC, captaining the side on their annual tour of Ireland. One year, Hammond asked, or was asked, to represent the MCC team on one such venture over the Irish Sea. His presence would boost the gate and do much to bash the Bible in a land that could be considered a bit of an outpost of the game. That is what these MCC tours did, and still do; they help to develop cricket in countries below Test level.

'He was a miserable sod,' said George of his star player. 'Instead of mixing with, and chatting to, the opposition and spectators, he just sat in the dressing room, gin and tonic in hand, silent and uncommunicative, offering nothing to his team-mates, many of whom were in awe of him. Far from uttering words of encouragement, his presence and demeanour were distinctly disagreeable, intimidating even. He wouldn't even come to lunch, seen as gross bad manners at these sorts of fixtures. A most unattractive person.' It ought to be said that these were harsh words coming from a schoolmaster famously mild-mannered and forgiving of human foible.

How extraordinary! Why should a man whom everybody admired feel constrained to act in such a fashion? What drove him to adopt such a jaundiced view of his fellow human beings and the society in which he moved? Was he naturally curmudgeonly, rude and unpleasant since childhood, or had something, or somebody, seriously troubled his mind? Did he, too, suffer from a lowering, debilitating, black cloud of depression? I was anxious to discover.

No psychotherapist neglects the beginning, where it all started. That was my uncomfortable experience, having parents, childhood, schooldays, socio-economic circumstances, the whole picture of those formative years, pored over and analysed.

Walter Reginald Hammond was born in 1903 at Dover Castle. He may well in later life, given his penchant for upper-class pretensions, have rather liked the romantic associations of being born in a royal castle but the reality was more prosaic. His father was a bombardier in the Royal Artillery and he and his wife lived in married quarters in the military barracks. The environment in which the young Walter grew up was the classical peripatetic existence of life in the army, nomadic and transitory. No sooner were friends made, and attachments formed, than the family was on the move again. Nothing was permanent. In his childhood, Walter lived in China and Malta before, on the outbreak of the First World War, the family moved back to England. It seems that his relationship with his father was distant. That was not necessarily a fault of parenthood, just the way things were in the military. His mother was a dutiful parent but lacking in emotional warmth. It was said that the young Walter never experienced any physical contact with his mother, in the way of hugs and kisses. She was of the stiff-upper-lip breed of mothers.

At the outbreak of the First World War, his father was posted to France while mother and child returned to England to live in Southsea. Wally attended Portsmouth Grammar School and while he was there, he was given news of his father's death, killed in action in Nantes in 1918. It is not to decry the emotional effect that this event had upon the young boy, but he was never close to his father. Furthermore, he was hardly unique; the loss of the man in the family was endured by hundreds of thousands throughout the land. We must look further afield for the reason for his depressed mental state later in life.

The young boy was sent away to board at Cirencester Grammar School soon afterwards. We can only surmise that his mother believed that a complete change was probably best for him. What is more difficult to unravel is the reason that Wally rarely returned home in the school holidays; for one reason or another, he preferred, or was told, to stay with friends at their house.

It would seem that Hammond troubled the scorers more than the examiners during his time at his new school. It was claimed that he scored 365 in a House match (coincidentally the exact same score that Garry Sobers managed when he set the highest individual score in a

Test match in 1958, a record once held by Hammond's 336* in 1933), which must have tested the poor scorer as much as the opposing bowlers and fielders. He was soon in the cricket first XI. Their fixture list was not an extensive one, mainly consisting of matches against local club teams. It was not long before correspondents of the local newspapers were filing glowing reports of the young prodigy. He left school, aged 17, with a less than glittering academic record but with stacks of runs to his name. He immediately turned out for Cirencester CC, scoring a century, news of which persuaded Gloucestershire to invite him to play for their Club and Ground side. It did not take long for the coach and the old pros to recognise his talent and to encourage the county to sign him up immediately.

That August in 1920, Hammond made his first-class debut against Lancashire at Cheltenham and remained in the Gloucestershire side for the remainder of the season. Scores of 0, 7*, 2 and 18 do not hint at future greatness but evidently the county were sufficiently impressed by his potential that he was offered a full-time contract. Playing professional cricket had not been the career that his mother had in mind for her son – she had envisaged farming as his occupation – so there was a certain amount of persuading on the club's part for her to change his mind. In the end she asked him outright, 'What do you want to do with your life, Walter?' to which he replied with just two words: 'Play cricket.' The die was cast.

Reporting for pre-season nets in 1921 was an eye-opener for the new boy. The county side, as many were in this era, divided sharply into amateurs and professionals. They changed in different dressing rooms, entered the field of play from different gates and were even segregated at mealtimes. Across the way, down the corridor and out in the middle, Hammond would have heard the clipped vowels of the strictly middle-class and patrician amateurs. Their accents and vocabulary would have been a world away from the down-to-earth, West Country manner of speaking that he encountered with his fellow professionals. Given his later class consciousness, some called it snobbery, he no doubt liked what he heard and rather fancied being like them too. Moderating, even changing, one's accent is a sure sign of an insecure social self-confidence and is a common occurrence as individuals seek to 'fit in'. In this regard, Hammond reminds me of the England football manager, Alf Ramsey. He strove to mask his working-class background by adopting a posher accent, a strange hybrid that was neither one thing nor the other. Hammond's background was distinctly blue-collar, but he hankered after the stiff white collars and bow ties of high society and the smart sets. By turning amateur later in his career, thus enabling him to captain England, he felt at last that he belonged in their company, a place that he should have joined from the outset, he believed, by virtue of his pre-eminence as a cricketer and the sheer weight of runs that he scored.

His progress, both socially and professionally was, for the time being, stymied by unbending officialdom, something he came to resent bitterly. A Kent supporter had noted that the debutant the previous season for Gloucestershire, namely one W.H. Hammond, had in fact been born in Kent. Obviously, cricket anoraks were as much in evidence in 1921 as they still are over 100 years later. For Hammond, the intervention was vexatious, to say the least. His place of birth was made known to the treasurer of MCC, Lord Harris, a renowned stickler for the rules, and a man of Kent, it should be noted (he had captained Kent and England in his playing career). He immediately slapped a ban on the player from playing county cricket, until such time that he had fulfilled the statutory two-year qualification period. Today, the rule and its implementation appear pettifogging and harsh but do not forget that, as recently as 1961, Tom Graveney was forced to spend a year in the wilderness before he was allowed to move from Gloucestershire to Worcestershire, and he was an England player!

It wasn't Hammond's fault that the club had not gone through the proper channels and done the requisite paperwork. There was no guarantee that an exception would have been made even if they had. The upshot was that he was not allowed to play county cricket in 1921 and 1922 at a crucial time of his development. Who can say how many more first-class runs he would have scored if he had been allowed to complete his apprenticeship at the coal face, so to speak? As it was, he was consigned to the second XI and to Gloucester CC for his cricket, spending the rest of the summer watching the first XI. He said later that this was a miserable period in his career, and he never forgave Lord Harris for the rest of his days, holding him totally responsible for the first of many perceived slights and injustices that he suffered throughout his life. 'I was livid,' he later wrote, 'and I was perfectly helpless.' Onlookers believed that thereafter in his county career, he always tried that bit harder against Kent.

This is not intended to be a biography of Wally Hammond; I am just trying to uncover possible triggers for his later black moods and deep depression. Was a slap in the face by cricket's hierarchy sufficient cause for emotional turmoil? Lesser wrongs have been known to disrupt mental equilibrium. But on balance, I think this was unlikely in

Hammond's case. He was still the same gauche young man who re-joined the team two years later. During the winters of his 'qualification' period for Gloucestershire, he played football for Bristol Rovers. Unsurprisingly for such a gifted sportsman, he was a pretty decent player. As a winger, he possessed the attribute that all defenders dread – pace – and it was the considered opinion of more than one contemporary that he could have played for England had he trained harder and taken it more seriously. But cricket was his preferred occupation and always holding him back was the fear in the back of his mind that he would suffer an injury that would prevent him playing the game he loved. Incidentally, he could hit a golf ball a mile, and he played off scratch. He accepted a bet from his team-mates to see who could hit it the furthest. Hammond placed his tee in the middle of the centre circle of the old Eastville Stadium and proceeded to hit the ball way over the stands, hitting the gantry of a nearby gasworks. Nobody bothered to take him on.

In many ways the life of a professional cricketer, with its disciplined routine and class divisions, was not unlike the world of an army barracks, where he had spent his childhood. His social horizons started to open up, he began to attend dinners and dances and he joined a tennis club. Slowly it dawned on him that the world of the middle-classes, throwing off the shackles of a narrow, pre-war morality (these were, after all, the Roaring Twenties), was very much to his taste. He even bought himself a car, a necessary aid for any putative philanderer, a label that soon moved from 'putative' to 'acknowledged'.

The term of his ban having expired, in 1923 he set about making a name for himself on the cricket pitch as much as on the dance floor. He scored his maiden first-class century that summer against Surrey and though he did not reach three figures again that season, he did impress many an experienced journalist and administrator. In the end-of-season report, *Wisden* said of him: 'Hammond has all the world before him and there is no telling how far he may go.' He had started taking wickets too and it was felt by his club and by onlookers that he could be classed as a genuine all-rounder. The following season, he scored 250* against Lancashire, repeatedly hooking the Australian fast bowler, Ted McDonald, in a display which Neville Cardus reckoned was 'one of the best innings that can ever be accomplished by a boy of his age'. Now the England selectors sat up and took notice.

It was no surprise that Hammond was picked for the MCC tour of the West Indies that winter. At the time, a tour of the islands was seen very much as a social merry-go-round and Hammond, still no more than a boy don't forget, was determined to enjoy himself. And enjoy himself he most certainly did, both on and off the pitch. He scored 732 runs at 48.80 including a chanceless 238* against the full West Indian side. Furthermore, to took 20 wickets at 38.65 and was by far the most athletic fielder in the party. His running and throwing often brought gasps of admiration from the large crowds. In the evenings, he threw himself with gusto into rounds of dinners and dances where the young daughters of the plantation owners were a constant attraction. Not to mention the casual availability of the local women in the larger cities, who assumed that the England players were wealthy young men and game for some fun. The young Wally was more than game.

The first public stirrings of concern and bewilderment about Hammond were raised as the SS *Ariguanii*, on her maiden voyage, docked at Avonmouth in the Bristol Channel, bringing the MCC tourists back from the West Indies. As the bronzed cricketers made their way down the gangplank, there was no sign of the figure that everybody had come to see. Where was Wally? Eventually he appeared. His mother, who had come to meet him, was shocked at his appearance. He had lost weight, he was wan and listless, and he was visibly weak. He explained that he had been bitten by a mosquito, which had left him feverish and agitated. Immediately, on their returning home, his mother summoned a doctor who, after the most perfunctory physical examination, contacted Gloucestershire, to seek permission for their young star to be admitted to a local nursing home. By this time, Hammond was running a dangerously high temperature and was delirious.

Things got worse rather than better. One of his legs had become dangerously inflamed and the talk among the doctors was of possible amputation, which his mother, to her credit and belatedly to the nation's gratitude, flatly turned down. Various interventions and procedures were carried out but to no avail. The fact was that the doctors just didn't know what was wrong and indeed where to start looking.

By now, the 1926 season was well under way and the question on the lips of the Gloucestershire faithful and cricket supporters throughout the land was not where was Wally, but what was wrong with Wally. The official press releases and communiques from the county were vague and gave little hint of how seriously ill he was.

Of course, now we know the nature of his illness. The smokescreen released by those in authority is perfectly understandable given the social mores of the time. Syphilis since time immemorial has been the disease that dare not speak its name and the censorious world of cricket committees and MCC would have wanted to sweep the truth about the rising star of English cricket under the carpet. Even now, I doubt any current international player would freely admit he is being, or has been, treated for the disease. In my career in the 1970s, several contemporaries, some of them household names, were suspected of having 'a dose of the clap', but nothing was ever publicly acknowledged. There were hints, veiled references, cloaked allusions, winks and nudges about what happened on that tour amongst Hammond's team-mates but very little escaped into the public domain. It was a huge stigma to bear and Hammond's, and the club's reticence was wholly understandable.

Hammond's treatment in the West Indies had been basic and flawed from the outset and back in England it was not much better. In terms of medication at this stage of medical research, what he was probably prescribed had not greatly changed from the Middle Ages. He would have been treated with the customary injection of arsenic and mercury. 'Two minutes with Venus and two years with Mercury' was the ironical, cynical saying of the time.

The point of my scrutiny is not to cast censure on Hammond's behaviour – he was, after all, a young man still naive of the ways of the world – but to consider whether his illness, or at least the treatment of it, had any bearing on his subsequent depression. What are the mental and psychological, to say nothing of the physical, consequences of the disease? Would any of this explain his later fractious and querulous behaviour?

According to my brief research, I gather that there are three stages to syphilis. The primary stage of infection typically presents with a sore or chancre to the sexual organ, something in Hammond's case that could easily have been explained away by a mosquito bite. In the second stage, a rash appears, often accompanied by high fever, sore throat, weight loss, malaise and fierce headaches. We can assume that this was how Hammond was feeling on the boat journey home. Tertiary infection includes, among other symptoms, inflammation anywhere on the body, with the central nervous system affected, which can result in dementia, personality changes, delusions and depression. Abrupt changes in mood are also symptomatic of this stage.

At what point Hammond's doctors suspected the true nature of his illness and started the time-honoured treatment for the disease, we shall never know. Now, of course, that remedy is discredited and has been superseded by the use of antibiotics, specifically penicillin. But no such relief was available for Hammond; penicillin was not discovered by Alexander Fleming until 1928 and did not come into general use until the 1940s.

It does not need me to point out that arsenic and mercury are poisons and can have severe side-effects. Mercury poisoning is known to affect the nervous system, resulting in mental, emotional and behavioural changes, including low self-confidence and depression. It was commonly called Mad Hatter Disease because it was a historical complaint of old English felt hat-makers who were exposed to the vapours from the mercury used to stabilise the wool.

I have been reading a biography of King George III. At various times during his reign, he descended into madness, usually attributed to the malady, porphyria. Modern science disagrees and argues that the king suffered from manic depression, now known as bipolar disorder. His physicians had no concept of mental illness. He was suffering from 'lunacy' and as such, he was subjected to the usual 'cures' of the time: bleeding, cupping, purging and even physical restraint, the use of the 'strait-waistcoat'. Historians now attest that the treatment the poor king suffered did considerably more harm than good. Hammond, alone and isolated in his room in the nursing home, wondering whether he was going to die (he was just 23), suffering torment from the disease and from its 'cure', must have been very a frightened young man. Did the 'cure' harm him more than the disease?

What is undeniably true is that he was a changed man when he finally emerged from his nightmare. His God-given talent for playing the game was undiminished when he resumed his career in 1927, after having missed the entire previous season. But team-mates noticed much in his personality that had altered from the fresh-faced, shy but pleasant-tempered boy who had first caught their eye before the ill-fated West Indian tour. Most notably, his complexion was different. It is difficult to assess in what ways because colour photography was in its infancy and all action shots of the time were in black and white, but the change was detected by those close to him. His skin tone was demonstrably darker. He had become withdrawn, not the shyness as in his youth, but aloof and unfriendly. In all the dressing rooms, cricket pitches and batting partnerships he shared, never did he offer any advice or encouragement to any of his team-mates. He became suspicious, almost paranoid, convinced that factions, both within the teams he played for and outside, were ganging up on him. Taciturn to a fault, he seemed to disappear within himself. Colleagues talked of long car journeys from cricket ground to cricket ground during which he did not utter a word. He became selective of the company he kept and, in adopting a new social circle, he felt it necessary to acquire an 'upper-class drawl', with specific verbal oddities and idioms particular to that group of people. He was accused of being arrogant and a snob and certainly that was not a baseless assertion. He was moody and solitary. It was said he had forgotten how to smile.

He may have forgotten how to smile but he had not forgotten how to play cricket. For the next decade or so, until the outbreak of the Second World War, he bestrode English cricket in the same way that Grace and Hobbs had in earlier eras. He was a pale shadow of his former self when he returned to international cricket after the war but that was not a unique experience. A whole generation of cricketers felt they had lost their best years to a world war. And let us not forget those who lost more than their way but their lives on active service, most notably former England team-mates of Hammond's, Hedley Verity and Ken Farnes. I think it is fairer to say that Hammond had lost his way, privately, long before the outbreak of hostilities.

Yet, despite his private demons, Hammond, season after season, continued to score runs and break records. Quite possibly, cricket, far from being the root cause of his mental struggle, became his salvation, a distraction, where he felt able freely to express himself away from his personal and social discord. His batting prowess identified him; with a bat in his hand, he felt invincible. He could take control, he was the master of the situation, nothing – none of his inner demons – could touch him. Only then, flaying the best attacks in world cricket, did he feel truly 'happy'. Fulfilled.

But as we all know. cricket is a fickle mistress and even such a masterful player as Hammond is subject to the whims and vagaries of fortune, mischance, Lady Luck ...

or what cricketers call 'form'. Furthermore, an opponent, a bête noire, who became a bitter enemy, started to cloud the waters until they were muddied and soiled, namely Donald Bradman.

Let us briefly cast our minds back over the significant achievements of the single Englishman who had any claim to be mentioned in the same breath as Bradman. On his return to county cricket in 1927, once he had recovered – physically anyway – from his illness, Hammond scored 1,000 runs in May, the first batsman since W.G. Grace to have done so. He very nearly scored 3,000 runs for the season and was named as one of *Wisden*'s Five Cricketers of the Year. He was a shoo-in for the MCC tour of South Africa. He made his Test debut in that series, scoring 51 and taking 5-38. Worn out after a long English season when he perhaps should have been taking things a little easier, he still averaged 40 for the Tests and took 15 wickets. He never looked back thereafter and even his 'barren' spell in the mid-1930s was hardly barren compared to others.

The Ashes tour of 1928/29 was a personal triumph. He scored 905 runs in the series at an astonishing average of 113.12, positively Bradmanesque, though he would have bristled at the comparison and was not best pleased when that record series aggregate was trumped later by The Don. In the infamous 'Bodyline' series of 1932/33, although his record stood comparison with anyone else's, it was noted that he did not enjoy a tit-for-tat barrage from the Australian fast bowler, Tim Wall, and was heard quite clearly to growl, 'If that's what the game's coming to, I've had enough of it!' Many Australian batsmen would have been inclined to agree with him. In 1933, he passed Bradman's record score of 334 and was heard to shout gleefully, 'Yes!' as he took the two runs to leave him on 336*.

In 1934, he fell ill with persistent sore throats and was also troubled with back problems, which probably explained his disinclination to bowl thereafter. His form suffered as a consequence. He had a poor tour of Australia, managing a top Test score of only 43 in the series. Another disappointing series against the West Indies provoked mutterings that his place in the England side might be in jeopardy, which was nonsense in view of his continued heavy scoring for Gloucestershire. His tonsils turned septic which necessitated their removal and the after-effects lingered as his patchy form continued in the South African series. All was restored to working order in the 1936/37 Ashes series in which he averaged 58.50 in a losing cause. The following season back in England, he passed Jack Hobbs's record number of Test match runs, a feat not equalled until Colin Cowdrey passed the milestone in 1970.

Then came the captaincy of his country and here Hammond's sensibilities about class coalesced with those of the country at large, certainly with the upper echelons of MCC. The very idea of a professional cricketer captaining England did not bear thinking about. But the idea of Wally Hammond, the best and most experienced player in the land, not captaining England also didn't bear thinking about. Ergo, Hammond had to turn amateur; the answer was as simple as that. So, with one bound, he could fulfil his social ambitions and take charge of the international team. In 1937, it was announced he was joining the Marsham Tyres board of directors, affording him a paid sinecure which would enable him to give up his status as a professional cricketer for Gloucestershire and henceforth play for them as an amateur. As sure as night followed day, he was then appointed captain of England, which led to some unkind comments that the world had come to a pretty pass when England was captained by a tyre salesman. Clearly, Hammond was not the only snob in the land.

The tasks of captaincy did not prove to be so onerous as to affect his batting; he averaged 61.76 in the 1938 series against Australia, scoring 240 in the second Test at Lord's, considered by those who witnessed it as one of his finest, indeed one of the most magisterial, of any ever played by an Englishman. There was little criticism of his captaincy as he seemed to handle his bowlers astutely. In the final Test at the Oval England won by the huge margin of an innings and 579 runs, thus drawing the series but not stopping Australia retaining the urn. England had amassed 903/7 declared, with Len Hutton taking away Hammond's world record individual score with 364 to his name. In that famous photo of Bradman extending a hand of congratulation to Hutton, it is significant that Hutton was accepting it because he had overtaken Bradman's score of 334, not Hammond's 336*. You see, the New Zealanders back then, against whom Hammond had set the record, were regarded as inferior opponents.

Mammoth totals were all the rage in these years. The winter tour to South Africa had to be brought to a premature end before the notorious 'Timeless Test', the last one of the series, could be finished. England were 654/5 at close of play on Day 10. The tourists would have missed their boat home. In any case, the war clouds were massing over Europe and cricket would soon become an irrelevance.

Whether strings were pulled because he was a famous sportsman and the England captain, it is difficult to tell, but there is no doubt that Hammond had an 'easy' war. He joined the RAF but as far as I can see he spent most of his time in Cairo organising cricket matches to raise morale for the troops in transit, either to or from India and the Far East. He attained the rank of squadron leader, but it is doubtful he ever led a squadron of men, certainly not in aerial combat. He also had time to travel to South Africa to play some cricket and to pursue amatory adventures.

It would be disingenuous to avoid a central pillar of Hammond's character – if I can put it like that – his many sexual conquests. He would not be the first, and unlikely to be the last, cricketer who had a failed marriage and a second one that did not prompt faithfulness on his part. Neither would he have been the first nor the last cricketer to have had a string of girlfriends, some out in the open, many clandestine. Two points strike me. First, with a love life as varied as his, it cannot have been possible that he lacked charm and charisma. All the stories about his curmudgeonly and moody personality came from men: team-mates, opponents, administrators, supporters, journalists, business colleagues. Evidently, he was a different animal in the company of women. Secondly, if he felt compelled to dally with so many women, he cannot have been a happy man, content with his lot and emotionally fulfilled with his partner. Contentment, seemingly, eluded him. Sex, like cricket, was probably an escape from his depression.

Who knows how many more runs he would have scored, how many more wickets he would have taken, how many more (effortless) catches in the slips he would have snaffled had not the war years intervened? It is a futile question. The same might have been said of Jack Hobbs had he not lost his prime years to the First World War, to say nothing of Hammond's nemesis, Don Bradman, a near-contemporary. On the resumption of county cricket in 1946, Hammond topped the national averages for the eighth time in succession and it was inevitable that he was asked to lead the MCC touring side to Australia in 1946/47. He shouldn't have gone.

Exhausted by war and much depleted in experienced campaigners, the England side were comprehensively beaten 3-0, with Hammond's form and health steadily deteriorating. Later, he admitted that he was close to a mental breakdown and on his return to England, he immediately announced his retirement from all first-class cricket at the age of 44.

What next? It is a question facing all those who leave the game, the rest of their life stretching out in front of them. Some cope better than others. Hammond moped and his steady deterioration was indeed sad to witness.

> 'How weary, stale, flat and unprofitable
> Seem to me all the uses of the world.'

These words were spoken by Hamlet, but they could well have come out of the mouth of Wally Hammond had he a poetic turn of phrase (which he hadn't). The only poetry associated with him was in his batting. The allusion to 'unprofitable' is particularly apt in Hammond's case. After retirement, he embarked on several business ventures. All of them failed. He was a hopeless businessman and was forever in financial difficulties. He died of a heart attack in 1965, aged only 62.

A lot went wrong with Hammond's life (though it has to be said that a lot went right too). Any one of his misfortunes might have driven a man to feel depressed; the cumulative effect of trouble piled upon trouble would have been hard to bear for even the most sanguine of personalities. And, as we know, Hammond was anything but sanguine. I have to admit for a growing. albeit grudging, sympathy for him the more I read about him. No doubt his syphilis, and the treatment prescribed for its cure, contributed to his melancholia and nobody, even his bitterest enemy (Bradman, incidentally, never regarded him as an enemy, no matter how intense their rivalry), would have wished that upon him. He certainly lacked human empathy and was undoubtedly a difficult man to live with. The milk of human kindness did not flow in his veins. But he was a tormented soul and as such, with our better understanding of mental illness, he is probably deserving of greater compassion than he was afforded in his lifetime. People remembered the majesty and the mastery of his batting but were pained by his flawed character.

I looked up (as if I had any need!) the symptoms of depression on the NHS website. Warning signs, among others, include feelings of unhappiness and hopelessness; persistent low spirits; restlessness, agitation, irritability; isolation and an inability to relate to other people. It seems to me that Wally Hammond, for all his athletic prowess, exhibited these symptoms in spades.

Chapter 5

When the Balance of his Mind Was Disturbed

Cricket's Suicides

'Suicide is a permanent solution to a temporary problem.'

A New York psychiatrist

WHEN ASSIGNED the task of writing the weekly essay by our tutors in the English department at university, we would normally be pointed in the direction of one or two seminal works or texts on the subject for research. The girls in the group would make an immediate beeline for the library; we boys would stop off at the coffee bar for some restorative refreshment, which would include for one of our number deep puffs on a spliff that he would surreptitiously roll with his back to the catering staff. I don't know why he tried to hide it; the smell – a familiar one to undergraduates in the late 1960s – was as obvious as gunpowder on Guy Fawkes Night. By the time we had made our way to the library, we were peeved that the sought-after books had already been signed out. How on earth were we going to do our 'research' and complete the essay? Desperation is the mother of invention; somehow, we found a way. There was a bright spark among us (the weed smoker), much more intelligent than the rest of us, who would come up with some original ideas and with a bit of horse-trading, he would share these ideas and we got the job done. An early lesson in teamwork, I always believed, excellent training for my future career as a professional cricketer.

In the same way that my tutors had guided me towards helpful 'reading around the subject', those who have encouraged me to undertake this task of writing about depression and cricket suggested several books that would be essential reading. The obvious one was *Coming Back to Me* (2008) by Marcus Trescothick, the one that set the ball rolling, focussing on his troubles and subsequent depression while touring with England. It was awarded the William Hill Sports Book of the Year, 'fearlessly tackling one of the great taboos of elite sport', as the citation put it at the awards ceremony. It is a fascinating, sometimes difficult, read and I think the adverb 'fearless' is indeed apt. If nothing else, the book has encouraged greater openness among past and present players, whose views I have sought and described, about their battles with this insidious illness.

By His Own Hand, written by David Frith, was another that passed across my desk. In it, he compiled a list of first-class cricketers who had taken their own life and explored their history and background in a quest to uncover reasons. I read it, engrossed and appalled in equal measure, greatly impressed by his scholarship and research. If suicide is the next logical step whilst mired in the dense fog of crippling depression, then surely these stories are pertinent to the subject of my book. Not one of my sources or subjects in my research ever denied that taking his own life had not at some stage crossed his mind even if, for one reason or another, he had decided not to embrace the ultimate quick fix. When I approached David Frith, telling him the nature of my project and asking him whether I could quote from his book, he reminded me that he had revised and updated his research in a new edition, *Silence Of The Heart.* At once, I recognised the quotation of the title as one from the French philosopher and existentialist, Albert Camus. I had studied his novels, *La Peste* (*The Plague*) and *L'Etranger* (*The Outsider*) for A Level French and I remember a whole lesson devoted by our enterprising teacher to Camus's essay on suicide, always an intriguing topic for self-obsessed adolescents. I looked it up again:

> 'There is one truly philosophical problem and that is suicide. Judging whether life is or is not worth living amounts to answering the fundamental question of philosophy. An act like this is prepared within the silence of the heart, as is a great work of art. The man himself is ignorant of this. One evening he pulls the trigger or jumps.'

I am not at all sure what we sixth-formers made of all that, except that we were aware that Camus, a more than useful goalkeeper before tuberculosis curtailed his career at 17, believed in the essential absurdity of life; man's existence is totally devoid of meaning. He wrote extensively about the subject of suicide, seeing it as a natural, logical solution to the utter pointlessness of life. He was killed in a car crash in 1960, aged 46, thereby quite possibly saving him from answering his own existential questions.

When my wife, a social science graduate, was proofreading this chapter, she urged me to look up the work of one of the three major sociologists of the late 19th century, Emile Durkheim, a Frenchman. The other two were Max Weber and Karl Marx, both German. Durkheim's studies helped to establish the academic discipline of social science. One of his theories centred around suicide. He used scientific tools such as statistics, surveys and historical observation in his analyses of the rate of suicide among the Catholic and Protestant societies in France at the time. He concluded that there is more to suicide than personal circumstances, such as bereavement, loss of job, divorce and bankruptcy. He argued that data proved that the rate of suicide was greater among Protestants than Catholics. Why? Catholics wrap themselves around the comfort blanket of belonging – to the Church. There is a greater social cohesiveness in this group. Protestantism, by its very nature (the clue is in the name), rejects the communion of worship; man must face his God individually, without the intercession of priests, bishops and popes. There is less social control. Thus, Durkheim postulated that lack of cohesion between people – 'group attachment' – and lack of regulation of behaviour are responsible for suicide more than individuals' feelings and motivation. 'There you have it,' my wife said. 'You mean that only Protestant cricketers commit suicide, not Catholics?' She knew I was being obtuse. The point she was making was that ceasing to belong to a group, a cricket team, has been scientifically proven to be a plausible explanation for suicide.

Frith's point, at the conclusion of his book, is that cricketers are like artists. 'But cricket is an art, is it not? Who would deny that it too lies in the silence of the heart, emerging to enchant, to torment, to consume?' I believe that to be true. What game more perfectly embraces the beauty of its executio? Think of the action of a fast bowler, a Fred Trueman or a Dennis Lillee or a Michael Holding, pure poetry in motion. Or the elegance of Tom Graveney's cover drive, or a Barry Richards back cut, or a David Gower on drive. Or the subtlety and hidden menace of a sharply turning ball from Shane Warne. These were performers, as cherished for their style and elegance as much for the runs they scored or the wickets they took. Even the most ordinary of us players have known that apogee of perfection, albeit fleetingly, at some stage in an innings or a spell of bowling. Yes, cricket is an art form and as we know, artists are fragile people. As it used to be said in the Malvern College common room, 'The Art Department is a law unto itself. They do things differently over there.'

So, I read Frith's updated version, *Silence Of The Heart*, and it is indeed a sorrowful catalogue of cricket's lost souls. The thing that struck me most was the slew of reasons for their ultimate, self-destructive act. Many were the vicissitudes of life and random tragedies that assailed them. Rarely were they spontaneous acts. They were often planned, with suicide notes – not always logically written which is understandable under the circumstances – left for posterity. What is undeniable is that retirement, either self-induced or forced, from cricket leaves a void that many struggled to fill. Once you have quit the stage and no longer experience the roar of the crowd and the smell of the greasepaint, what else is there to live for?

Since writing *Silence Of The Heart*, Frith told me, 'I have unwittingly become identified as something of an "expert" on the subject. While nobody had ever researched it to such a depth, I would never claim to be any sort of "clinical expert". I'm merely a researcher and storyteller.' That may well be so, but Frith tells their stories honestly yet sympathetically, and as I was reading I became increasingly convinced that these men – and women – might have benefitted from some sort of earlier intervention. That is, if their distress was obvious. In many cases, it was not. It is only in recent years that opening up about mental illness has become acceptable … and advisable. One can imagine, given the prevailing understanding, or lack of it, at the time that they would have preferred to keep their personal struggles to themselves. Sadly, to their great cost.

Most of the characters in Frith's book occupy no more than a footnote in cricket history, ordinary players treading the boards, so to speak, in repertory theatres throughout the shires, with only occasional roles in the West End. Some were more than jobbing pros. Some were household names. Famous or unexceptional, all felt diminished in some way once the umpire had removed the bails for the last time. It seemed to me relevant for the purposes of this book to single out a dozen or so of the more pre-eminent among them to reflect on their inner demons and to consider whether their careers – successful ones, undeniably – contributed to their demise.

Albert Trott is best known for being the only batsman to have cleared the Lord's Pavilion with one mighty blow. It was hit off Monty Noble, the Australian, in 1899; ironic really, as Trott was himself Australian and it was one of the mysteries of the day that Trott, the finest all-rounder in the game at that time, was not playing for Australia. In the Ashes series of 1894/95, Trott had averaged 102.50 with the bat against England, captained by Andrew Stoddart, but was astonishingly omitted from the Australian touring party to England the following year. He sailed anyway on the same boat, but as a private individual, and qualified to play for Middlesex. Having taken 102 wickets in his first season, he was picked to tour South Africa in 1898/99 with MCC, playing in two Test matches, thus becoming the last cricketer to have played for Australia and England.

In 1899 and 1900, he was at his peak as an all-rounder, scoring 1,117 runs and taking 239 wickets and 1,337 runs and 211 wickets respectively. Quite clearly, he was an entertainer, very popular with the crowds. It was not unknown for him to share a glass of ale with spectators when fielding down at third man. He was amusing and a great tonic in the dressing room. Stories abound of his practical jokes. He was an unpredictable and entertaining cricketer; even such a scion of the ruling elite in English cricket, 'Plum' Warner, was visibly amused by his antics. Trott practised assiduously when young and his fielding was electrifying in an age when fielding at best was pedestrian. He smote the ball many a mile and, on wet wickets, he was practically unplayable. He took two hat-tricks in one innings in 1907 (actually, one of them was four in four), a feat that has only been equalled once. Sadly, following these peak years came a rapid decline. Trott's haul of wickets decreased as his alcohol consumption increased and he was finally forced to retire in 1911. Already gambling debts were crippling his personal finances and he abjectly commented, 'I've bowled myself into the poor house,' when he took that double hat-trick in his benefit match. Actually, this was not true – the match stretched into the third day and crowds had been good – but it was a gloomy assessment that probably sprang from a mental state that was already falling apart.

He was 37 when he retired and took up umpiring. He gave that up in 1914, as his health was declining. Sleeplessness and depression stalked him. Five days before the outbreak of the First World War, broken and alone, at the age of 41, he shot himself. The coroner found that he had taken his own life while 'of unsound mind'. He might have said, 'While unable to cope with life without cricket which defined him as a man.'

Andrew Stoddart was a truly glamorous figure in an era from the 1890s until the outbreak of war in 1914, known as the Golden Age of Cricket, populated as it was with numerous great cricketers who, it is fondly believed, played the game 'in the right spirit'. Their names roll off the tongue: Grace, Trumper, Blythe, Rhodes, MacLaren, Hobbs, Fry, Ranjitsinhji, Woolley, Foster and many others. Between 1888 and 1898, Stoddart, during which he played 16 Tests, captain in eight (when Grace was unavailable), could count himself one of that number. He also played rugby for England and was considered the finest wing three-quarters of his generation. In all he gained ten caps for his country, captaining the side in four of the internationals. He helped organise the first British Lions tour to Australia and New Zealand, taking over the captaincy when the original captain drowned in a sculling accident. He was a founding member of the Barbarians RFC and even turned his hand to Australian Rules football.

By all accounts, he possessed a fierce zest for life. A tale much in the telling recounts that when stumps were drawn at the end of play he played tennis, went to the theatre, danced the night away and played cards until dawn. His next match was against Kent. He scored a hundred. So much for curfews, proper sleep and careful match preparation. On one occasion, on a sunny day in August 1886, playing for Hampstead CC, he scored 485 out of a total of 813. The opponents, Stoics, returned home not having had a bat, as no declarations were permitted in those days. You have to feel for them. I hope their guests bought them a drink or two at close of play.

By the age of 35, Stoddart had lost interest in county cricket. Life working in the Stock Exchange provided none of the intense thrill of competition that he had enjoyed on the cricket or rugby pitch. His weight ballooned and he started drinking heavily. He was no financial whizz-kid and money worries assailed him more and more. His childless marriage was joyless, and he slowly sank into a pit of depression and despair. The suicide of his old Middlesex team-mate and friend, Albert Trott, affected him deeply. By 1915, on his own admission, he had reached the end of his tether. Apparently, he flourished a pistol in front of his wife, threatening to shoot himself. Later that evening, he carried out his threat. The coroner's verdict at the inquest was 'suicide, while of unsound mind'.

'If Stoddart was once the finest amateur batsman in the world, Arthur Shrewsbury, seven years his senior, must have been the best of the professionals.' This is the view of David Frith, one shared by no less an eminent judge than WG himself. Whenever he captained England and was asked what team he wanted, Grace replied simply, 'Give me Arthur!' In all, Shrewsbury played in 23 Tests, seven as captain (so much for the adage that professionals could not captain their country) and was the first batsman to score 1,000 Test runs. His batting was characterised by careful accumulation and judicious use of the pads as a means of defence (the old lbw law stipulated you could only be given out if the ball pitched between wicket and wicket). Descriptions of his style put me in mind of Sutcliffe, Barrington and of a more recent vintage, Boycott and Chanderpaul, all of whom eschewed extravagant strokeplay in favour of occupation of the crease. *Wisden* said this of him: 'Shrewsbury's batting was marked by extreme patience, unfailing judgement and a mastery over the difficulties of the ground of which probably no other batsman would have been capable.' On a sticky dog – and in the days before covered pitches, there were a few – he was without peer. His best years were in the 1880s but even in 1902, at the age of 48, he topped the national batting averages.

Opinionated and stubborn, which was reflected in his batting, he had an intense and uncompromising personality. Oddly enough, no doubt on account of premature baldness, he was never seen without his cap, even to team-mates in the dressing room, a sign perhaps that here was a man who was not wholly at ease with himself. Another indication of a lack of self-esteem and a propensity for depression and melancholy was that in middle age, he developed hypochondria. He complained of kidney pain, but the doctors could discover nothing amiss. As his powers as a batsman waned, he became despondent at the imminent end to his career. He said to his long-term girlfriend, 'I shall be in the churchyard before many more days are up.' He bought a revolver and, in 1903, shot himself. His first attempt was botched, only injuring himself in the side. At the second attempt, putting the gun to his head, he succeeded. The coroner's verdict was that he had 'committed suicide, his mind having been unhinged by the belief that he had an incurable disease', of which there was no evidence, the coroner added.

Aubrey Faulkner, born in Port Elizabeth, South Africa, played in 23 Test matches between the years of 1906 and 1912. He did make a 24th appearance for his country when the Springboks toured England in 1924 but whoever persuaded him to do so was a fool and the match, as far as Faulkner was concerned, was best forgotten. For at his peak in those halcyon pre-war days, he was arguably the best all-rounder in the world. At that time, some rated him as the best Test batsman and the second-best Test bowler. Certainly, his statistics would seem to bear this out, 40.79 with the bat and 25.58 with the ball. A prodigious schoolboy cricketer, he did not immediately play first-class cricket in the Currie Cup. There was the small matter of the Boer War to be fought. He joined the Imperial Light Horse in the Colonial Forces and saw action in the relief of Mafeking and Ladysmith. When hostilities ceased, he came home to play for Transvaal and it was then that he was taught how to bowl the googly by Reggie Schwarz, who in turn had learned it from Bernard Bosanquet, its inventor (hence the Australian term 'bosie' for a googly). Soon after, Faulkner was playing Test cricket and scored his country's first ever double-century. On their tour of England in 1907, South Africa possessed in their bowling attack a quartet of googly bowlers, Schwarz, Vogler, White and Faulkner, who terrorised England's batsmen throughout the series.

He was in England again for the intriguing, but ultimately unsuccessful, Triangular Tournament in 1912, featuring England, Australia and South Africa, the only three Test-playing nations at the time. The tournament was dogged by poor weather; the attendances – especially in the matches between Australia and South Africa – were disappointing and the venture was never repeated. The tournament may have been deemed a failure but Faulkner's contributions with bat and ball were anything but. At the conclusion of the series, Faulkner decided not to return home with his team-mates and remained in England in order to try his hand in county cricket with either Surrey or Middlesex. In the event, he was persuaded by a wealthy businessman to play club cricket in Nottinghamshire, which he did, with conspicuous success.

On the outbreak of the First World War, he joined the Royal Artillery and saw active service on the Western Front and in Macedonia and Palestine, taking part in the capture of Jerusalem. Promoted to major, he was awarded the DSO and Order of the Nile for his acts of gallantry. Malaria dogged him after the war, effectively ending his cricket career. To add to his unhappiness, his wife left him 18 months after his return to England. With the exception of the ill-advised single Test for South Africa in 1924 – he was answering an SOS from the national team, who were being slaughtered by a very strong England side – that was that as far as his playing days were concerned.

He opened a cricket school in Richmond in 1925. Its renown soon spread but it was a financial disaster. A popular man, with an outwardly genial manner, he suffered greatly from lack of funds. One of the reasons put forward for the financial woes that plagued his business, despite its popularity, was that he was too kind and modest to set fees at a realistic level. A teetotaller himself – his father had been an abusive alcoholic – he refused to have a bar on the premises, which further reduced potential revenue. He worked himself to the bone to turn things around, but all to no avail. Beset by depression, he gassed himself in the storeroom in 1930. He left a suicide note; 'Dear Mackenzie, I am off to another sphere via the small bat-drying room. Better call in a policeman to do investigating.'

David Foot, his biographer, called **Harold Gimblett** 'the tormented genius of cricket'. His story gives full credence to this description. Gimblett was born in Somerset in 1914 and his first-class debut for his county in 1935 became the stuff of legend. He was having a two-week trial at the County Ground but had failed to impress. The secretary called him in to inform him that he simply wasn't good enough but decided that he might as well see out the remaining days of the fortnight and pick up the 35 shillings for his pains, as well as the bus fare home. On the last day of Gimblett's trial, Somerset found themselves one man short, a not altogether unusual predicament for one of the less fancied and less wealthy clubs in the Championship. Gimblett was told to report to Frome for the match, but he missed the bus and had to hitch a lift on a lorry. By the time he arrived, Somerset were already in trouble. When he made his way out to the middle, they were in even deeper trouble, at 107/6. Gimblett immediately set about the Essex bowling, hitting 100 in 63 minutes, which proved to be the fastest century of the season. He was eventually dismissed for 123, with a mere 52 runs coming from the other end. Somerset cantered to an innings victory.

Fame was instant. He was 'the coming man' in the game, whose promise was rewarded by selection for England the following summer against India. He played in two Tests but did not enjoy the experience. 'Thank goodness that's over,' he remarked when news came through that he had been dropped. He returned to Somerset, where he felt more at home, harbouring deep resentment, oddly enough, for his lack of success on the international stage and being summarily discarded. He had another of his purple patches in 1939, which prompted the selectors to pick him once more for the national side in the first Test against the West Indies. Opening the batting with Len Hutton, he scored 22 and 20, not enough to keep him in the side for the subsequent matches of the series. Then war broke out.

He volunteered for the RAF but was instead assigned to the Fire Service. No sinecure, this; he witnessed awful scenes whilst on duty when Plymouth and Bristol were heavily bombed. Back with Somerset after the war, he was the mainstay of their batting for a good eight years. But character flaws, already hinted at as a young man, became more noticeable. He was clearly not an easy man to share a dressing room with; several of his team-mates would be the butt of his unkind and barbed comments. To the outside world, including Somerset supporters, he presented a cheerful countenance, in keeping with his swashbuckling manner of play. To those closer to him, the personality he revealed was full of contradiction and private resentment. According to Foot, Gimblett had complexes about class, privilege, wealth and health and seemed to be driven by a hatred of many things. An entertainer in the middle, back in the pavilion or at home, a grouchy and morose character reasserted itself. He was waylaid by regular bouts of depression. Despite his obvious talents and abilities as one of the most attacking batsmen of his day he was frequently racked with anxiety and fear of failure. He seemed no longer to be enjoying the game and, as he got older, and the spectre of retirement loomed ever closer on the horizon, his mood, always morose, became more and more gloomy.

At the conclusion of the 1953 season, he suffered what can only be described as a full mental breakdown. He spent 16 weeks in a psychiatric hospital and underwent a course of electro-convulsive therapy. He found it difficult to return to county cricket the following season and it was obvious to all, players and administrators at Somerset, that he was a spent force, emotionally and physically shot. His parting with the club, his home for the best part of 20 years, was far from amicable.

Predictably, retirement brought little in the way of personal contentment. He took the professional role at Ebbw Vale CC, then was taken in by his former captain, Jack Meyer, the founder and headmaster at Millfield School, where he was given a variety of jobs. But he eventually fell out with the school, as he seemed to fall out with everybody. Bitter and resentful at the malign hand of cards that fate had dealt him, he took an overdose of prescription drugs and died in 1973, aged 63. In his career, he scored over 23,000 runs, with 50 centuries, often in a weak Somerset side that offered him scant support, yet he was unable to reconcile his former fame with the craven manner that he believed the world had treated him.

Sid Barnes, regarded by many as one of the finest Australian batsmen in the immediate post-war years, was an integral member of 'The Invincibles', the team led by Don Bradman, which went through the 1948 season in England unbeaten. In fact, as the youngest of the team, Barnes had made his Test debut before the war, in England during the 1938 Ashes tour. As with so many other first-class cricketers, his career was stalled during the war. He enlisted in the Second Australian Imperial Force but saw no action. Bored with the rules and routine of life in the military, he sought permission, which was granted, to join a firm which built tanks, putting his trade background and business skills to good advantage.

Once cricket started up again in earnest, he soon, by sheer weight of runs in the Sheffield Shield, returned to the Test team, though by now, he had eschewed his former flamboyancy of strokeplay in favour of crease occupation. He started to grind out the runs and was thus promoted to open the innings to accompany Arthur Morris. According to Barnes, it was Bradman who had suggested this change of approach, and it certainly paid dividends. In the second Test match at Sydney during England's tour of 1946/47, he made an indelible mark on Ashes history. Together with Bradman, he set a world record partnership of 405 for the fifth wicket, a record that still stands today. Bradman was eventually dismissed for 234 and four balls later, Barnes was out, also for 234. It was no coincidence, Barnes later claimed; he couldn't possibly have exceeded Bradman's score. Alec Bedser, who bowled Barnes 'with a beauty', always scoffed at the idea. 'So,' announced Barnes with a twinkle in his eye, 'my name would always come above Bradman's because of alphabetical order.' None of his team-mates would have put it past the mercurial, unpredictable fellow. He was a genuine eccentric, who seemed to cause controversy wherever he went.

Tales of his unorthodox behaviour and contempt for authority were legion. Dubbed by one cricket correspondent as the Artful Dodger, Barnes certainly lived up to the tag; he was an inveterate practical joker. He once came out as a 12th man, dressed in a suit, carrying cigars, iced towels, mirror, comb, brush and a radio. In Bradman's testimonial match, he came to the wicket and took guard with a miniature bat. When an lbw appeal was turned down, he seized a stray dog and presented it to the umpire, with the words, 'Now all you need is a white stick.' He was the archetypal wide boy, always on the look-out for the main chance, uncaring about criticism or disapproval. He infuriated England batsmen by standing fearlessly at short leg or silly point, right under their nose, usually scuffing up the pitch in the process. Understandably, he was unpopular with cricket's hierarchy, who objected to his high jinks, particularly so when he brought a libel case (unsuccessful, as it turned out) against the Australian Cricket Board in an attempt to get himself reinstated in the Australian team following his retirement in 1948.

So far, so larrikin, one might be tempted to say. But there was a darker side to Barnes, for all his high spirits and high scoring. He was stubborn and self-interested. Following his cricket career, he did well in business but increasingly paranoia took hold. He started to have nightmares, accompanied by panic attacks. Periods of deep depression followed. He sought psychiatric help and agreed to undergo several sessions of electro-convulsive therapy. Slowly, all his friends melted away and he admitted to his family that life held little interest for him anymore. This was a man who had played 13 Tests for Australia, straddling the Second World War, finishing with a batting average of 63.05, outstanding in any era. But the memories were not enough. Perhaps they were too painful. In 1973, he committed suicide by an overdose of barbiturate drugs. He was 57.

For a very brief period, between 1949 and 1951, **Jack Iverson** held the cricket world in his grip. Or rather, his fingers. To be precise, one finger, the middle one of his right hand. There is always something intriguing and captivating about spin bowling of the highest class. Fast bowlers, genuinely fast bowlers, elicit visceral feelings of aggression and menace; the fear, the possibility, of physical danger adds to the gladiatorial spectacle, which onlookers find compelling. Facing a fast bowler is a test of character and technique. Whatever private misgivings that swirl around in a batsman's head, he must not show fear, or he will be ruthlessly exposed. And then we get a spin bowler who takes a couple of paces to the wicket and lobs up a gentle delivery that totally flummoxes the batsman. The contrast could not be more marked. Fast bowling scrambles the nerves. Spin bowling scrambles the mind. Mystery spinners capture the imagination even more because they are so rare and because we have always been beguiled by illusion and wizardry.

At school, Geelong College in Victoria, Australia, Iverson was a fast bowler. He stopped playing when he left and did not take up the game again until 12 years later and it was a further 15 years after that before he made his first-class debut. On active service during the Second World War in Papua New Guinea, during idle moments, he would amuse himself by playing with a ping-pong ball, developing a flick with his middle finger, 'as if disposing of a cigarette butt', as Frith memorably described it. After the war, he developed his 'specials', as he called them, with a tennis ball. Once he had perfected the trick, he tried it with a cricket ball, most successfully, it turned out. His rise thereafter through the ranks in grade cricket was meteoric until he found himself making his first-class debut for Victoria at the age of 34. That season, 1949/50, he took 46 wickets at an average of 16.12. Nobody, even the best state batsmen, knew how to play him. With this unique flick of the middle finger, he was able to bowl off breaks, leg breaks and googlies without any perceptible change of action. The following season, he was picked for Australia and played in all five matches of the Ashes series against England, led by Freddie Brown. The Englishmen could make no more head nor tail of his bowling than his fellow Australians. His success in the series was astonishing. In all, he took 21 wickets at the low cost of 15.73.

Many years later, Richie Benaud, a 'leggie' himself, offered this assessment of spin bowling: 'There have been plenty of spin bowlers around for more than 100 years, but for me, who have broken the mould and made batsmen think seriously about what was coming down the pitch at them, have been Bernard Bosanquet, Jack Iverson, John Gleeson and Shane Warne.'

But if Iverson's rise was meteoric, his fame burnt out as rapidly as it had appeared. A large, shambling man, with no pretensions as a batsman, he lacked confidence, and his head would droop if ever he was carted. Convinced that his 'mystery' had been rumbled, he simply gave up playing, appearing for Victoria only once during each of the next two seasons, before packing in the game for good. Fear of failure and disappointment had crippled him. Later, he ran an estate agency and did a few stints commentating on the radio. In his early 50s, he developed severe clinical depression as the pressures of work took their toll. He became silent and uncommunicative and submitted to electro-convulsive therapy, which had little beneficial effect. Badly let down in business, he simply gave up on life as he had given up on cricket. He shot himself in the chest in his garden shed, aged 58.

I remember **Jim Burke** from the notorious Ashes series of 1958/59, which England lost 4-0, firmly believing that the Australians fielded four bowlers with suspect actions. 'Chuckers', they were labelled. Jack Fingleton, the former Australian opener, agreed. Wittily, he called his book on the series, *Four Chukkas to Australia*. I gained a privileged insight into the atmosphere in the England dressing room from Tom Graveney when I was writing his biography. 'They were all chuckers,' he said. 'Ian Meckiff we called Ian Chuckiff. The worst offender was Gordon Rorke. He would run in, stop about 18 yards away because of his excessive drag, raise himself to his full height of six foot four and simply throw it at you. Colin Cowdrey used to joke that he was more afraid that Rorke would step on his toes.'

In point of fact, Burke did not bowl in this series; his action was considered so blatantly suspect that it wasn't risked. All I can say to that is that it must have been *extremely* suspect to be unfavourably compared to the others. But he did bowl in Sheffield Shield and grade cricket and took a stack of wickets. It was said that he got away with it because he was such an affable man and used to chat up the umpires shamelessly. For Australia, he was more of a batsman who bowled – I use the word loosely – occasional off breaks. Throughout the 1950s, he played in 21 Tests, in and out of the side, though he did top the Australian batting averages in England in 1956, when Jim Laker took 46 wickets in the five-match series. Burke was in truth a stodgy batsman but away from the pressures of the international arena, he could play in a pleasing and attacking style.

He was a popular and humorous man, who kept team-mates and friends entertained with his jokes and piano playing. But life after cricket grew increasingly cheerless. His second marriage was on the rocks and operations on his dodgy hips threatened his beloved golf. Over and above these personal setbacks, financial problems were crowding in. At the time of his death, a disastrous investment had left him in debt to the tune of $150,000. The sad irony of it all is that had Burke held his nerve, the investment was later turned on its head and he would have become a wealthy man. But, as it was, seeing no way out, he purchased a shotgun and shot himself through the heart. Poignantly, Frith quotes in his book a famous saying by a New York psychiatrist: 'Suicide is a permanent solution to a temporary problem.'

Burke's suicide at the age of 48 rocked the world of cricket, most notably because none of his many friends had any idea that behind his big smile and jovial exterior lay a personality plagued by self-doubt and private torment. We are all actors, those of us who suffer from depression, and some of us are consummate actors. Burke was clearly one of this number; 'His nature,' wrote Frith, 'had seemed so inviolably sunny.' If nothing else, his suicide prompted much soul-searching among the cricketing fraternity; the statistics were beginning to speak for themselves.

Frith's story of lost souls who have taken their own lives now becomes more personal – for me, at any rate. I did not play against **Stuart Leary,** but I did against several of his team-mates, who remembered him fondly and spoke about his humorous antics. Leary was born in South Africa but came over to this country to sign professional terms for Charlton Athletic FC. He was a prolific goalscorer, making 403 appearances for the club throughout the 1950s. In the summer months, he played cricket for Kent between 1951 and 1971 and was a member of the Championship-winning team in 1970.

Following retirement, he returned to his homeland to take up several coaching positions but already the dark days of depression were becoming a constant companion. He lost his job as coach of Western Province. It was the opinion of a former team-mate of Leary's, Bob Woolmer, that the heavy-duty, anti-depressant medication that Leary had been prescribed contributed to his dismissal. Woolmer argued that the drugs may have stopped Leary from killing himself, but they also changed his character and thus he became less effective as a coach. Alas, the staying of the hand of suicide was only temporary. Leary bought a ticket to go up Table Mountain in Cape Town on the cable car, walked to the edge of the cliff and threw himself off. His body was not discovered until three days later. When I asked a couple of former Kent players with whom I had kept in touch about his death, they still wanted to believe that it had been a terrible accident, that he had lost his footing or something. How could such a fun-loving man want to kill himself? Admitting eventually that the evidence was overwhelming, the uncomfortable realisation dawned on them that – once again – nobody knew. It was not the done thing in dressing rooms of that era to admit to weakness and human frailty.

David Bairstow was not just a name from the cricket history books; I knew him, having played against him several times in the 1970s. He always struck me as a loud, irrepressible presence behind the stumps, never shy of a comment or opinion about your batsmanship, rarely complimentary, but I took it all as the normal Punch and Judy, rough-and-tumble species of male banter. It was never personal.

He was Yorkshire born and bred and with that mop of red hair (oddly nicknamed 'Bluey') he was never going to be a shrinking violet on the cricket field. He played for Yorkshire throughout his 21-year career, totalling 459 first-class appearances and almost as many one-day games. He played only four Tests, seemingly in the eyes of the selectors well behind Bob Taylor and Paul Downton in the pecking order of England wicketkeepers.

My impression of him as a boisterous, rumbustious sort of fellow was not misplaced. Even his friends saw him as frank in his opinions and opinionated in his utterances. He was blunt and to the point and was not above argument and confrontation. Yet he was honest and there seemed not to be a dissimulating bone in his body. He captained Yorkshire from 1981–84, during which he had run-ins with the committee and the manager of the team Ray

Illingworth, but all were agreed that he gave everything for the cause of Yorkshire cricket. Some worried that he put so much of his life and soul into his game that he would have little left to spare for himself when he retired. As often is the way with cricketers who only know cricket, those characters who have little hinterland beyond the game, he firmly believed he could play on for a couple more seasons, which he patently could not.

When the time came to put away the gauntlets for good, he was at a loss. He dabbled in public relations; he worked in sports merchandising, and he acted as a summariser on the radio. None of it greatly appealed. Despite his rough good humour, depression set in, and problems mounted. His second wife was being treated for cancer. A car accident had left him with a badly damaged arm, which had put paid to his golf. Business troubles chipped away at his peace of mind and an impending court case – for speeding, most likely resulting in a 12-month driving ban – hung like a black cloud overhead.

In late 1997, he took an overdose but survived. In typical bluff manner, he claimed that he had not really intended to kill himself, insisting that he was fine. He was not. In January of the following year, his wife found him hanged at their home. He was 48.

The cricket world well beyond the borders of his native Yorkshire was stunned. I did not know him well, but it was still a shock; he seemed indestructible, both on and off the field of play. Evidently, that was not the case. He was at a loss, unable to cope with life without cricket, depressed and unhappy, and despite appearances to the contrary, he was as fragile and as destructible as the best of us.

Peter Roebuck, I always thought, was an 'odd 'un', as they would have said in his native Somerset. Of all the cricketers I have played with or against, he was the one I could least fathom. I did not know him well but even his Somerset team-mates, though accepting of his idiosyncrasies, never really got to the bottom of his singular personality. When Hampshire played against Somerset sometime in the mid-1970s I observed his behaviour over the course of the three days with interest, soon developing into puzzlement. This had nothing to do with his ability as a batsman. Though slightly ungainly at the crease, he was an accomplished run-getter, scoring over 17,000 runs in 335 first-class matches. He also bowled tidy off-spin and didn't drop many at slip. No, my observations were of his interaction, or total lack of it, with the rest of the team. Throughout the Hampshire innings, he did not exchange a word with any of his team-mates. Conversation, not always of the most erudite nature, between slip fielders is almost *de rigueur*; after all, long hours spent in the field can be monotonous without a bit of light relief. He was slightly aloof in the dressing room too, according to my sources. The Somerset lads were not put out. There were plenty of loud and boisterous characters in that team to cope with somebody who chose to remain detached. His lofty demeanour was put down to his intelligence, the fact that his mind was probably operating on a higher plane to everybody else's. That he was brainy is indisputable. Both his parents were teachers, his father of economics and his mother of mathematics, who were offered employment at Millfield School by the unconventional headmaster, Jack Meyer, the former captain of Somerset, in order that they could afford to send their son to the school. Apart from being a gifted sportsman, the young Peter was something of an academic prodigy. He won a scholarship to Emmanuel College, Cambridge, taking a first in law. He never practised law, however; the lure of a career in professional cricket and latterly as a writer and commentator on the game proved overwhelming.

Controversy seemed to stalk his life, despite the fact that the gods had seemingly bestowed on him a rich bounty of talent and gifts. Perhaps we should have been more alert to the signs of incipient mental turmoil that bubbled to the surface even in the early days. He wrote the entertaining and instructive book *It Never Rains – A Cricketer's Lot*, which chronicled Somerset's season in 1983. It was a personal account, recording the ups and downs of the team's performances as well as the vagaries in his own form. Some of what he wrote makes difficult reading, especially in view of what happened to him subsequently. 'Almost every season I sink into a trough of despondency which lasts sometimes a week, sometimes a day. For some reason, I seem unable to last from April to September without a bout of morose self-examination. I can sense a growing upheaval within, and I am afraid it will not easily be stilled.

'I wanted to be as I am in the winter and cannot be during the season. There's no threat in the winter. I cannot be undermined. Nothing can go terribly wrong and there's no need to tense myself to avoid cruel failure.'

By the time of the great internecine war at Somerset in 1986, I had long quit the game, but I watched on, fascinated, as the club seemed to be tearing itself apart, with characters whom I knew well snarling at each other's throat. Passions were aroused, animosities brought to the surface and positions became deeply entrenched. Much blood was left on the floor. At the conclusion of the 1986 season, Roebuck's first as captain, Somerset had finished an ignominious second from bottom of the County Championship. He decided that the two overseas players, Joel Garner and Viv Richards, were past their sell-by date and needed to be shown the door. He wanted to invest in a policy of youth. A brave move I thought at the time; Joel Garner was an immensely likeable and popular player and of course Richards was a towering legend of the game. Ian Botham, a great friend and ally of Richards', threatened to leave the club if they were sacked, a threat he carried out when, following a great deal of in-fighting amongst committee and members, the contracts of the two West Indians were not renewed. In one sense, Roebuck's initiative paid off; there was an immediate improvement in Somerset's performances the following year. But friendships had been fractured, never to be repaired. Famously, Botham never exchanged another word with his former team-mate, even when they came across each other in later years, in press rooms, TV studios and hotels. Already, it seemed, Roebuck was a divisive figure.

He retired from professional cricket in 1991, though he continued to have a very successful career in Minor Counties cricket, captaining Devon for ten years. In the meantime, he carved out for himself an enviable reputation as a cricket journalist and commentator. I admired his writing. It was fluent, perceptive, intelligent and interesting. His was a peripatetic existence, flitting between England, Australia and South Africa.

Then came that strange court case in 2001. He had invited three young South African cricketers back to England for coaching at his home and at his expense. Criminal charges were brought against him for common assault, to which he pleaded guilty. He had laid down house rules and if any of these were broken, he would subject the culprit to a caning. The press had a field day. All the ingredients for a juicy story – latent homosexuality, corporal punishment, public school bullying – were present in abundance. Roebuck was given a suspended jail sentence but with his reputation in tatters, he fled this country and thereafter divided his time between Australia and South Africa. What an odd fellow, those of us who knew him were left musing. My impression, admittedly from afar, was that here was a man who had not truly rediscovered himself once total immersion in playing the game had come to an end.

That impression was reinforced when I was in Australia in 2003/04 visiting our son on his gap year and taking in some of the series between Australia and India. Watching on the television, I was intrigued by the identity of one of the commentators. Over time, you become familiar with the sound of their voices and can pretty easily identify who is who. This voice I could not pin down. When his name was mentioned, I was, quite frankly, shocked. It was Peter Roebuck, but instead of the well-modulated vowels of a Cambridge graduate, we could only hear a fair dinkum Aussie accent. When I made this point to others in the press box whom I knew, they said that when he was in South Africa, he adopted the clipped vowels of a native South African. I shook my head in bafflement. You expect young children to mimic the accent of whatever domestic situation in which they find themselves, but a grown man, well into middle age …?

When the news of Roebuck's suicide in 2011 filtered through, I was struck by the words of his former Somerset team-mate, Vic Marks, when asked for his reaction to the distressing bulletin. Marks sucked in his breath and admitted that though it had come as a shock, it was not altogether a surprise. The intimation was that there was always a dark side to his old friend (Marks was one of the few of his Somerset contemporaries who kept in touch), something hidden which nobody had been able to figure out. The circumstances surrounding the suicide were equally murky. Whilst Roebuck was in Cape Town commentating on the South Africa versus Australia Test match in November 2011 he was approached by a member of the South African police, who wanted to interview him about an alleged assault on a 26-year-old Zimbabwean man. Roebuck asked to go up to his room on the sixth floor to get changed. He climbed up to the window and hurled himself out. I know that hotel and I know where that room is. Looking down, there is nothing but concrete below. Roebuck died instantly.

The details about Roebuck's so-called philanthropic guardianship of young Zimbabwean students, with rumours of sexual misconduct, beatings and hints of blackmail, do not really concern us here. It is the nature of the man that intrigues. He had so much going for him but evidently personality flaws stalked him and ultimately brought about his downfall, literally so. He shared little of himself, everybody who knew him was adamant about that. He feared, so associates said, that if he did, nobody would understand, his reputation would suffer; that he could not bear.

Could the blame for Roebuck's death in any way be laid at cricket's door? That question is less easy to answer than those of other stories I have highlighted. Certainly, in his cricket career, a successful one, we should not forget, Roebuck felt he was in control and could score runs, which validated him, and as a captain (of Somerset and Devon), he could mould a young team in his image, once again in control of things. It is hard to escape the conclusion that Roebuck led a double life; the hidden one driven by forces he could not control but which left him with feelings of deep self-loathing. On the point of being exposed (for the second time), he took the only course open to him ... and jumped.

There is a sad irony that for the first edition of *By His Own Hand*, David Frith asked Roebuck, by then an established writer himself, to pen the foreword. Roebuck's words strike a chord, one closer to home than perhaps even he realised at the time: 'Cricketers are supposed to be simple, even gung-ho, in sexual matters, as in everything else. And yet cricket – and most cricketers – has its dark secrets, its skeletons.' His book, *It Never Rains*, has a deliberate paradox in its title. Well, of course it rains during a season – we all know that. The paradox seemed to me to be Peter Roebuck himself. 'To me,' he said later of the book, 'it was a way of saying goodbye to all that. Once written, it was no longer true of my life.'

Perhaps, it would not be too fanciful to use the metaphor of a cage – a gilded one undoubtedly – for Roebuck's life as a cricketer. Within that cage, he was able to be himself, quirky, self-obsessed, but with a talent he was happy to explore. He felt secure and valued. Once he stepped out of that cage, he was exposed, vulnerable, unable to cope, not at all sure who he was anymore. His activities after he retired only brought passing satisfaction and he became more prone to succumbing to the darker forces of his personality.

> *Our natures do pursue*
> *Like rats that raven down their proper bane*
> *A thirsty evil and whenever we drink, we die.*
>
> Measure for Measure (Shakespeare)

Claudio likens humans to rats that 'raven down their proper bane', that is, rats that devour poison. In other words, we humans cause our own suffering by not having sufficient self-knowledge. It's hard not to think that Roebuck, for all his academic brilliance, did not really know himself.

I know Esher railway station. Many years ago, I alighted there from the Waterloo train to play in a schoolboys' representative match. London Schools. Or was it Surrey Young Amateurs? Or perhaps my club, Beddington? The opponents and the match did not live long in my memory; all I can recall, as I lugged my unwieldy cricket bag to the bus stop, is that I was determined to get myself some wheels at the earliest opportunity. Cricket gear and equipment, as every player knows, is a large hindrance in transit. Esher CC is a delightful ground, set deep in leafy Surrey, with a pavilion fronted by a white picket fence.

All these long-forgotten memories flooded back to me when the dreadful news emerged that Graham Thorpe had stepped into the path of an oncoming train at Esher station. I was immediately reminded of that famous photograph of him, white bandana around his head, arm in arm with Nasser Hussain, walking off the pitch having secured England's 'win in the dark' at Karachi in 2000. How had it gone from elation at a famous victory to taking his own life in such horrific circumstances 24 years later? He had the respect and affection of countless team-mates and opponents, he had had a successful coaching career, he had a loving wife and two adored children ... what could possibly have gone wrong?

Since the news broke, just as I was putting the final touches to this book, I have been continually asked whether I knew Graham. I confess that I did not; our paths never crossed. All that I have been able to discern about the tragedy has been gleaned from press reports and eulogies from those who knew him. Or thought they did. Not for the first time, it crossed my mind that nobody knows what goes on in another's brain. His act of self-destruction clearly came as a shock to his immediate family, let alone his friends and former team-mates.

A shock perhaps to his wife but probably not altogether a surprise. She has gone on record as saying that her husband had suffered from acute depression for years. He had made an attempt on his life two years previously and had been sectioned and placed in intensive care. No explanation was given at the time for his hospitalisation but now his wife has decided it was best to tell the whole story. 'He was so unwell in recent times,' she said, 'and he really did believe that we would be better off without him, and we are devastated that he acted on that and took his own life … mental illness is a real disease and can affect anyone. Despite having a wife and two daughters whom he loved and who loved him, he did not get better.'

The questions pile up. Why? Why? Why? Was cricket to blame, the nature of the game and his abrupt removal from the England team after 100 Tests in the same summer as the Greatest Series Ever in 2005, in which he took no part? Or was Graham temperamentally drawn towards introspection and feelings of inadequacy, a successful international batsman who achieved the pinnacle of his profession through a combination of physical prowess and mental strength, but now felt cast aside? Once the cheers and applause faded away, what was left? Had he given the game his all and had no more to give? These are questions that will be mulled over in the coming months and years. For now, Graham Thorpe joins a ruinously long inventory of cricketers who have 'died by his own hand'. His death adds to the swelling chorus demanding answers and action over the mental health of cricketers. I wish I could feel more sanguine that the magic bullet will be discovered. That is if such a 'cure' even exists.

Roebuck died after *Silence Of The Heart* was published, so he does not number in the 151 cricket suicides that the author has identified. Frith does not merely present us with a potted history of their life (and death) but asks questions and seeks answers about their personality and circumstances and the possible connection with cricket. He poses the same question as I have at the beginning of this book. Does cricket, more than any other game, attract those susceptible to introspection and depression (and possibly suicide) or does the cruel nature of the game affect its players? In short, is cricket to blame? The answer to that, I think he concludes, is that there is no answer. Or not one that can be commended with absolute certainty. Each one of us is different and nobody else can truly know what is going on in our mind, even if we can confidently say that we know (which often we don't).

Man's frailties are inbred, says Frith. Disillusion in later life happens to a lot of people, although it can be said that disillusion among cricketers comes earlier. Most of the suicides that Frith has studied seem to have been occasioned by outside influences, yet it is undoubtedly true that these unfortunates felt cast adrift when, for whatever reason, their careers came to an end.

The nature of the game, Frith readily accepts, is not a great vehicle for mental equilibrium. All games are subject to chance, to luck, to happenstance, but cricket, more than most, can be a cruel mistress. It takes a strong character to accept being run out for a duck at the non-striker's end by an unlucky deflection and then sit in the pavilion for the rest of the day and not rail at the merciless gods for having abandoned him. Superficially, cricket is a team game, but it is a lonely place at the crease; the odds, as well as 11 opponents, are against you. And nobody runs alongside you as you run up to bowl; the ball is in your hand and nobody else's. Frith makes the point that 'cricket's virtues are renowned. Played well it gives thrilling satisfaction to both performer and spectator.' County or club cricketer, we all have had our moment in the sun. But think of a spell of bowling by Jimmy Anderson, when he appears to swing the ball late at will – both ways. Or Shane Warne weaving his web of guile and mental ascendancy. Or an innings of Barry Richards, each stroke a masterpiece of orthodoxy and elegance. These performers raise the game to an art form; that is what makes cricket so enchanting.

Furthermore, for those who play it, professional or amateur, cricket provides a fellowship, a family; the dressing room is a safe and comforting shelter. When that protective tent is removed, the winds that blow are fierce and bitter 'and a void is created which at its worst can be fatally damaging'. Frith goes on to point out that 'half-hearted cricketers are extremely rare'; we are all fanatical about the game, so its loss is hard to bear. The suicides that he writes about were all beset by a number of problems in their life: bad health, money worries, alcohol dependency, marital strife, the sort of heartaches and perplexities that can ambush us all until the 'mounting depression became overwhelming'. The jury is out, he concludes, as to whether cricket is entirely to blame but he admits that the undeniable tensions of the game are undoubtedly a contributing factor. Only the strongest can put down their career and look to the future.

Frith knows of what he speaks. In his book, he admits he was close to despair when *Wisden Cricket Monthly* dispensed with his services for no apparent reason after 17 years' service, in which he had poured his heart and soul into the magazine. 'By the grace of God, I stopped short of considering, let alone planning, self-extinction but I tremble to think how near that fatal step I actually might have been.' He also poignantly told me that he had endured some terrible dark nights of the soul after his wife died after 62 years of marriage.

As a postscript to his research into cricket suicides – though he is adamant there will be no additional inquiry on his part; that is a ball someone else will have to pick up – he confided in me that India is the great untold story of the distressing problem; reports of suicides among young cricketers in that country are only now emerging. The popularity of the game in India, especially in the wake of the craze for the IPL, 'has led to countless youngsters falling apart when coaches have dropped or ignored them, crushing their dreams'. As always with that vast, teeming subcontinent of harsh extremes, the sheer numbers boggle the mind, but Frith's point is sadly all too credible.

I have always – somewhat flippantly – attempted to make sense of the essential absurdity of life by comparing it to an innings – there is always one ball with your name on it. Or as Frith puts it, 'Time beats us all.' Shakespeare, as ever, had the right words: 'Everyone can master a grief but he who has it.'

Chapter 6

A Brief History of Depression

'I would consent to have a limb amputated to recover my spirits.'

Dr Samuel Johnson

I GAVE a sharp, involuntary intake of breath during that famous episode in *Blackadder*, when Samuel Johnson, the great man of letters, (played by Robbie Coltrane) is importuning the muddle-headed Prince Regent (played by Hugh Laurie), to sponsor his great work, *A Dictionary of the English Language*, only to discover that the half-witted Baldrick (played by Tony Robinson) has used the manuscript as kindling. Of course, we know that never happened. But the point is that it could have. Famously, the historian, Thomas Carlyle, sent his only copy of his *History of the French Revolution* to his friend, fellow philosopher John Stuart Mill, to read and comment, only to be told that Mill's servant had used it to light the fire. Undaunted, Carlyle proceeded to re-write the entire book from scratch.

It is doubtful that Samuel Johnson had backed up his work on a hard drive, or indeed that he had made a time-consuming copy. Had the manuscript found its way into the fire – heaven forbid – the despair experienced by the writer could only be imagined. For Johnson was a depressive and the careless loss of his *magnum opus* would more than likely have tipped him over into suicide, a last resort that at times in his troubled life seemed a not unattractive option.

It is not easy for us in a later age to comprehend what a colossal figure of the 18th century Johnson was … poet, playwright, essayist, moralist, critic, biographer, editor and lexicographer. The *Oxford Dictionary of National Biography* refers to him as 'arguably the most distinguished man of letters in the English language'. Of course, it is his dictionary for which he is most famous, an outstanding achievement of scholarship, which took him seven years to complete. Hitherto, there had been widespread dissatisfaction with the standard of current dictionaries, a blot on the literary landscape, as a rise in the literacy of the general public demanded better standardisation and categorisation of the English language. Johnson's towering masterpiece remained in general use until the publication of the *Oxford English Dictionary* 175 years later.

So why have I opted to single out Samuel Johnson's battles with depression when history is littered with famous characters who likewise suffered? Without recourse to any research, we can reel off a string of names: Lincoln, Newton, Freud, Twain, Dickens, Woolf, Beethoven, Tolstoy, Churchill. There were many others. The reason for my fascination is that Johnson straddles the seismic shift in philosophy, metaphysics, doctrine, beliefs – and medicine – from the religious superstition of the Middle Ages to the Renaissance, the Age of Reason and the explosion in science and discovery. It is ironic that Johnson, the patron saint of logic and reason, should have been consumed with the myths and theology of the old beliefs, that the afterlife encompasses divine punishment for sin, a fate to which he firmly believed he was destined. In other words, before him came the pre-scientific world of melancholia and after him came the verifiable certainties of modern science, a movement from the heart and the soul as repositories of human emotion to the mind, from the ancient humours of the body to the electric impulses of the brain. Johnson was no sportsman by any stretch of the imagination but as I have been informed on countless occasions, depression is no respecter of age, class, sex, race ... or even athleticism. Yet a brief examination of his life might throw up similarities of background and common personality traits that are recognisable to all sufferers.

Whatever drove Johnson to heights of genius can be traced back to his need for perfectionism as a child. If you think about it, cricket demands perfection, of delivery and shot, ball after ball, for a lengthy period until an effective spell of bowling or a satisfactory innings has been achieved. And, as we all know, the duration of that spell of good form is all too finite. Johnson was frequently dissatisfied with his perceived deficiencies which persisted throughout his life, despite his later fame and acclaim. It was a long life, and his depression came and went with varying degrees of severity. As a student at Oxford, his literary output was prodigious but invariably he was pessimistic about its worth. As his success grew, he became more and more convinced of the 'vanity of human wishes', and the pointlessness of human achievement. In this regard, he brings to mind the existentialist writers of the early 20th century, such as Jean-Paul Sartre, Simone de Beauvoir, Albert Camus, Franz Kafka and Samuel Beckett, all of whom believed in the essential absurdity of life. Therefore, there is no meaning, no purpose, to our existence. Not a bundle of fun reading their works.

Johnson was consumed by guilt, of many things but one he readily admitted was the guilt he felt at the death of his wife (who was 20 years older than him) whom he had shamefully neglected. Furthermore, he suffered grievously from religious guilt, that he was an imperfect human being, and that divine retribution would eventually subsume him. Guilt and anxiety are unholy bedfellows and are frequently connected to depression. His brother, who also suffered from depression, had committed suicide, which only added to his despair, that somehow, he was singled out for damnation. At times, these feeling of worthlessness were overbearing and for a while, he lost himself carousing in the pubs and clubs of London.

To his credit, he battled hard with his depression. As he got older and more successful, he was better able to 'manage my mind'. His great companion and his famed biographer, James Boswell, describes in detail the conversations he had with his subject, advising exercise (plenty of it), distraction, company and above all 'talking through' feelings of anxiety and worthlessness. This does not feel a million miles away from the 'talking therapy' employed by counsellors and psychotherapists of today. Johnson turned his back on drink as the solace for his ills and thereafter concentrated on 'distractions of the mind'. Boswell records his friend's words in his *Life of Samuel Johnson:* 'When I survey my past life, I discover nothing but a barren waste of time with some disorders of body and disturbances of the mind, very near to madness.'

Anybody who has suffered from this debilitating condition will heartily echo every word.

If we take Samuel Johnson as a sort of Janus, looking back to the ancients and their understanding of the world whilst at the same time casting eyes into the future of science and learning, it is probably advisable to consider how we got where we are today. *'What is past is prologue,'* observes Antonio in Shakespeare's *The Tempest*, meaning that history sets the context for the present.

From as far back as Hippocrates, the Greek physician of classical times, known as the Father of Medicine, it was believed that the human body comprised four humours: blood (sanguine), yellow bile (choler), black bile (melancholic), phlegm (phlegmatic). These four substances were organised around the four elements – cold, hot, moist and dry – as well as around the four seasons (the planets and their positioning to one another also played a part). If you have a preponderance of blood in your system, you are likely to be sanguine – of an optimistic, positive, cheerful disposition. If yellow bile in your constitution is in the ascendency, then you are likely to be choleric – bad-tempered, irritable, irascible. If black bile dominates, then melancholia asserts itself. If phlegm is predominant, the likelihood is that you will be calm, placid, unemotional. These Ancient Greek words (though 'sanguine' derives from Latin) remain understandable to us today. A healthy body and mind meant that there was a nice balance of these four humours in your constitution; any imbalance caused illness and mental perturbation.

Modern medical science has of course blown these theories clean out of the water, as misguided, often harmful, hypotheses, not much better than black magic, alchemy and the worst excesses of quackery. Yet, for all that, we have to admit that there is a certain beauty in the symmetry and logic of it all.

In the absence of any credible alternative, no wonder it gained such traction over millennia and became the complex discipline that occupied the greatest minds of succeeding generations.

Our matter is depression. However, the term 'depression' is a relative newcomer as an epithet for bleakness of mood and even now it is subjected to re-assessment, as not being wholly fit for purpose, covering a multitude of symptoms and possibly misleading. We have already discussed the distinction between somebody who is 'depressed', a little bit down-in-the-mouth, fed up and temporarily low in mood, and somebody who is 'clinically depressed'. There is a world of difference. From classical times to the 20th century, depression was known as melancholia. Too much black bile in the body.

Hippocrates characterised melancholia as 'fear and despondency that lasts for a long time'. Other symptoms include loss of appetite, sleeplessness, irritability, agitation and listlessness. It was another Greek philosopher, Aristotle (famously the tutor of Alexander the Great) who first linked melancholia to genius. What made men depressed, with feelings of inadequacy, made them restless to achieve. Just take another look at that list of great men who suffered from depression at the top of this chapter.

Broadly speaking, these ideologies of melancholia survived into and through Roman times, except that Galen, a Greek by birth but who served under successive Roman emperors, Marcus Aurelius, Commodus and Septimus Severus in the years AD 167–217, added the state of anguish, delusion, unexplained fears and uncontrolled tears to the growing list of symptoms of the illness.

Christianity was a game-changer in the interpretation of the cause and nature of melancholia, as it was in all walks of life. A two-pronged attack on the illness, so to speak, gradually developed. Purging (the use of bleeding, vomiting, laxatives, diuretics) to rid the body of excess black bile (melancholia) was allied to spiritual assistance (prayer, confession, penance, scourging). The body and the soul needed cleansing. Melancholia was a problem for mediaeval religion. If it could not be cured, then the only possible explanation was that the patient was possessed of the devil. Either that, or the suffering endured was the result of God's anger for a sinful life.

As alchemy gave way to chemistry and the secular slowly replaced the religious during the Renaissance of the 16th and 17th centuries, the concept of the humours was superseded by a greater understanding of the human body, made up as it is of nerves, fibres, blood, arteries, lungs. Flows of internal fluids can be blocked, chemicals in the body can become unbalanced; there must be an understandable *reason* for a patient's suffering. Magic, superstition, astrology, supernatural power, sin, the devil, no longer satisfied the more questioning thinking of the time.

Melancholia became socially fashionable; men and women were willing to announce themselves of having at least a touch of the melancholic disposition. We are all aware of the disaffected young man frustrated in love or ambition, so common in the literature of the time; artists, composers, actors, poets, writers, who mope around the place, questioning their self-worth and stricken with a lassitude that precludes any meaningful action. Hamlet is a classic case. Grieving for the death of his father, lamenting his mother's 'o'er-hasty marriage' to his uncle (his father's murderer), he seeks proof of foul play in his father's death. When provided with the proof he craves (by virtue of his father's ghost appearing before him), he somehow finds himself incapable of taking the revenge that is his by right, descending into deeper and deeper gloom, introspection and self-doubt. His existential question, 'To be, or not to be,' must be the most famous quotation in the English language.

In another of Shakespeare's plays, *As You Like It,* Jaques scoffs at the melancholic who is very much *a la mode*: 'I have neither the scholar's melancholy which is emulation, nor the musician's which is fantastical, nor the soldier's which is ambitious, nor the courtier's which is proud, nor the soldier's which is ambitious, nor the lawyer's that is politic, nor the lady's which is nice, nor the lover's which is all of these.'

His may be a sardonic take on the subject of melancholia, but it doesn't make it any the less real for the sufferer. Each person's inner torment is individual to him or her alone.

It was now accepted that men and women irrespective of class and background display symptoms of depression, anxiety and despair. These symptoms are familiar to us today though their understanding of how the body and the mind function are not. We are leaving behind the world of humours and are embarking on a journey of science, albeit one that is not yet fully understood or explored.

The Age of Enlightenment brought about a radical change in Western intellectual tradition, which moved from a deductive and intuitive approach, broadly speaking springing from religious or superstitious beliefs to more empirical, observational, scientific hypotheses. The period of rigorous discourse of science, politics and philosophy in the 18th century, one which valued measuring, quantifying, observing and searching rather than taking things on blind belief and superstition, gave melancholia yet another definition and interpretation; it was a disorder of the nerves. The doctor now became more important than the priest in its treatment. By the time of Queen Anne, the term 'melancholia' had largely been replaced by 'hypochondria', 'spleen', 'hysteria', 'vapours'. At first, following Isaac Newton's laws of motion and universal gravitation, the body was likened to a hydraulic machine with a network of pipes and nerves, which sometimes, like all machines, springs a leak or malfunctions. Neurology, the branch of medicine that deals with the diagnosis and treatment of disorders of the nervous system, was all the rage. Melancholy was a nervous indisposition of the brain caused by a fault in the system.

The discovery of electricity by Benjamin Franklin in 1752 and its rapid spread for a variety of uses opened the way for its possible benefits in treating melancholia, or whatever term was favoured by whatever practitioner at the time. The nerves, electrical impulses, delicate, refined, gossamer-thin pathways could be carefully readjusted using electric currents passed through the body – the precursor of electro-convulsive therapy, still in use today. Alongside these theories, the discipline of psychiatry became a popular phenomenon, a more patient-friendly, sympathetic and persuasive treatment to discover the source of the problem, such as great loss, childhood trauma, shock to the system and emotional upheaval. This too could be seen as the precursor of today's talking therapies.

By the time of the early 20th century, the term melancholia had largely been replaced by the catch-all term 'depression', derived from the Latin '*deprimere*' or '*depressare*', 'to press down'. Who or what was doing the pressing, and why, remained a matter of debate. The end of the Victorian period in many minds meant the end of melancholia. We were now moving away from the perception of melancholia as a disorder of the emotions to that of the intellect. The idea that the patient had been seized by some despairing passion, and that passion becomes the dominant element, no longer held water, any more than did the passing fad of the water cure.

What was indisputable was that the loss of God in Western civilisation was central to arguments about depression, as it was in all philosophical thought. Writers such as Camus, Kafka, Beckett, Ionescu and Pinter saw life as inherently absurd and human suffering as inevitable. If you do not believe in God and possible divine forgiveness at the Day of Judgement, the world can seem a very bleak place. The answer surely was logical analysis, a rational examination of man and his place in the universe. This more reasoned thinking was encapsulated by Sigmund Freud, who believed that the patient was suffering for a reason; that is why he burrowed around in the subconscious to discover a loss or a shock in childhood, resulting in repressed anger towards self. Psychoanalysis was now the way forward.

The scene was now set for the explosion of the mental health market in the second half of the 20th century. The concept of pathological sadness was based on a biological model which was amenable to Prozac, the magic bullet for depression. This period was one of drug treatments, driven by the pharmaceutical companies. Depression was caused, it was now generally accepted, by a chemical imbalance in the brain, which could be cured, or at least ameliorated, by a bespoke drug regime.

Has the magic bullet hit its target? Has the proliferation of tranquillisers and anti-depressants been as effective as was first claimed? It seems, from recent evidence, that patient experience has been variable. The widespread use of Prozac has had a mixed press, so that some psychiatrists are now openly questioning the value of drug use, wondering whether the mental health sector is in thrall to the pharmaceutical companies. If Prozac and its many cousins have been discredited in the eyes of some – but not all – practitioners, what are the alternatives?

At this point, I feel that I might be sufficiently informed to give an answer, for the very good reason that I have been through, at one stage or another, all four therapies that are currently at the disposal of psychiatrists. There is electro-convulsive therapy, a controversial procedure but still in use because it seems to work on some patients, though the doctors who recommended it in my case were not at all sure why. The drug regime on which I was placed is also a case of spraying bullets far and wide, in the hope that one or two might hit the mark. Barely a month goes by without another drug coming on the market and it must be difficult for doctors to withstand the positive promotion that the pharmaceutical companies put out. After all, the latest anti-depressant might just work, and who would want to be the one who ignored it? The drugs work for some people, so who are we to scorn them? Cognitive Behaviour Therapy (CBT) is a talking therapy that seeks to unravel your thoughts and behaviours in order to help you change some of these to manage your problems. In other words, if you can identify your negative thinking patterns that you feel trapped in, there is a better chance of breaking out of this vicious circle. *I feel bad. It's all my fault. I should be stronger than this. But I feel guilty because I can't.* All of us who have suffered from depression will readily recognise the symptoms. Once again, this method does not suit everybody but because some are resistant is no reason to abandon it. Mindfulness is the latest of the beguiling healing elixirs. It encourages the patient to live in the moment and not reflect on the past (full of errors) or look to the future, which is unknowable and therefore worrying. It is used to reduce stress and to manage panic attacks, as well as to feel happier and calmer when the inevitable storms of everyday life strike. *Now, tell me – well, tell yourself – what happened today that gave you pleasure? It could be the smile of a grandchild. It could be the smell of recently cut grass. It could be the first sip of coffee of the day. Hang on to that thought because that is what makes life worth living, no matter how small and insignificant.* Once more, it is hard to argue with that objective.

So, what have we learnt on this journey from Hippocrates to GlaxoSmithKline? We have progressed from a preponderance of black bile, a concept that spanned millennia, from classical civilisation to mediaeval times, which in turn gave way to the more modern understanding of depression (though, as we have noted, this term is far from specific and occasionally misleading). Yet, in spite of all this progress, are we any nearer to identifying a reliably validated disease and its cure?

In many ways, it could be argued that we have come round in a large circle. The modern vision of the whole person rather than a biological unit is arguably a return to the Hippocratic concept of the affliction. No longer do the experts believe that depression is exclusively a disease of the brain. Just as important in diagnosis is an examination of the patient's life experience, which could have contributed to inertia and a lack of interest in life. The thinking and feeling patient should be at the heart of any therapy. And the Hippocratic remedy to ameliorate the symptoms of depression – regular sleep patterns, sensible diet, plenty of exercise, positive mindset – ring as true today as they did in ancient times.

Does that mean there has been a total break from the biochemical model, that the magic bullet of Prozac has been wildly off-target? Not necessarily, goes current thinking, because drugs do seem to work with some people. But the new approaches to melancholia are more prepared to focus on the social and personal psychology of the individual. So, far from identifying a 'cure', which science purportedly will always do in time, some psychiatrists believe that the recent history of depression shows significant *regression*, not progression, in understanding the most basic distinction at the heart of the illness – the difference between normal sadness and a depressive disorder. We are no further on, it is claimed, from Hippocrates, who defined depression in terms familiar to us and who did draw a distinction between sadness and depression. 'Fear and despondency that lasts for a long time' was his description. It's a question of degree; the length and severity of the attacks seem disproportionate to the rational mind. That was melancholia. That is now depression.

It was Donald Rumsfeld, the US Secretary for Defence, who uttered the unforgettable phrase 'the known unknowns'. I believe he was speaking about the Iraq war and the existence of weapons of mass destruction. At first, I judged the words to be no more than meaningless gibberish, often favoured of politicians, especially American ones. His boss, President George W. Bush, uttered hogwash on more than one occasion. But the more I considered Rumsfeld's words, the better I understood what he meant. The more you discover about a matter or issue or problem, the more you realise how little you know and how much is still dark and hidden. This could just as well be applied to the philosophical and psychological pursuit of the cause and a cure for depression. Clinicians today are armed with copious amounts of scientific data and evidence, but they seem no closer to a thorough understanding of the illness than Hippocrates. This is the nature of empirical research,

I guess. One theory is propagated with accompanying statistical evidence. It is then challenged, discredited and further research is undergone, with yet another theory submitted. And so, the cycle of human enquiry and exploration continually evolves. (This is reason in abundance that scientific investigation should never be held in secret; true wisdom and scholarship should always be held up to public scrutiny.)

There is a glimmer of light amidst all the gloom. One indisputable benefit of modern analyses of depression is that the stigma attached to mental illness, widespread for centuries, is slowly being erased. To quote once more the hoary old cliché, beloved of counsellors everywhere: 'It's OK not to be OK.' But that is not the end of the story, not by a long chalk. Public opinion takes some shifting. Treatment for depression is the subject of impassioned debate among the experts and even patients have their pet theories and prejudices. Alternative theories and treatments have proliferated and the efficacy of drugs, not so long ago the holy writ of treatment, no longer has total public approval.

In the meantime, there is little else for the sufferer to do but to battle on, using what tools and strategies that are available and suit. There is no cure, no natural panacea, no magic bullet. For some, it is a daily struggle. It's hard to answer the question – what's wrong when nothing is right.

A grief without a pang, void, dark and drear
A drowsy, stifled, unimpassioned grief
Which finds no natural outlet or relief
In word or sigh or tear.

Samuel Taylor Coleridge

Chapter 7
Injured Minds

'The game spares no one.'

Jonathan Trott

I HAVE been reading a historical account of the battles on the Western Front during the First World War. The commanders involved, the tactics and strategies adopted, the details of trench warfare, the industrial amount of munitions and shells expended in what was rapidly turning out to be a war of artillery, even the advent for the first time of tanks on the battlefield … all this makes for fascinating – if sobering – study. But of course, what shocks to the very core is the unimaginable number of casualties. On practically every page is an estimated figure of the dead, wounded and missing. You keep having to pinch yourself; surely there are one or two too many zeroes in those totals. But no, the sheer scale of the human cost is staggering and almost too much for the mind to grasp.

Then a thought took hold. Physically wounded men are easy to identify and straightforward to count. But what about the mentally scarred? Do they count? *Were* they counted? You see images of soldiers on the front line, their faces hollow and expressionless, the empty stare in their eyes. The concept of 'shell shock' was only fitfully understood and treated during the First World War; during the Second, the condition 'battle fatigue', as it was then called, was better acknowledged and it had become accepted that even battle-hardened troops can only endure front-line combat for a finite period of time. Today, we refer to the condition as 'post-traumatic stress disorder' and specialised treatment for those afflicted is now firmly established. The brain, the mind, the spirit is not immutable; it is subject to wounding just as much as any other part of the body.

It would be far-fetched – and in any case wholly inappropriate – to draw a parallel with the suffering of depressed cricketers, both past and present, and the wholesale slaughter of millions on the Western Front. Yet there are undeniable echoes to be picked up by those with an ear to listen. The very language that we use in cricket is shot through with military imagery. We talk of doing battle with the enemy, campaigns, bombardments, thunderbolts, missiles, helmets, lines of attack, batteries of quicks, counter-attacks, fighting fire with fire. I remember the description of the Indian dressing room on their tour of the West Indies in 1976 as resembling a casualty clearing station. The West Indies had only taken 11 legitimate wickets to win the Jamaican Test; the rest were either retired hurt or in the Accident and Emergency Department of the local hospital. Several of the Indian batsmen had clearly lost their nerve.

Cricket is a hard game, hard to master and played with a hard ball. The mental disintegration of its players from time to time does indeed find its corollaries in shell shock, battle fatigue and PTSD. On their return from the bruising Ashes tour of Australia in 1974/75, several England players admitted they were on occasions in fear of their lives in the face of an unrelenting pace barrage from Dennis Lillee and Jeff Thomson. One of them privately admitted to me he was mentally shot, and he was never the same player subsequently. His inner torment could only be imagined.

Of course, it is not only fast bowling that scrambles the mind. Spin bowling can play havoc with one's wits. Shane Warne had the Indian sign over many a fine batsman, ironic really, because most of the best spinners have indeed been Indian. Sometimes, it is one particular bowler who gets inside a batsman's head. Famously, an Indian trundler, by the name of Eknath Solkar, got under the skin of Geoffrey Boycott; so disorientated was he that he took a three-year, self-imposed break from Test cricket. Kevin Pietersen, who could destroy the best attacks in the world, strangely suffered from attacks of nerves against left-arm spinners, even the most innocuous. Or it could be a batsman who plays havoc with a bowler's confidence. Whenever Hampshire played Gloucestershire and Mike Procter strode to the wicket, our very own left-arm spinner, Peter Sainsbury, would throw the ball back at our captain and flatly refuse to bowl. 'Can't bowl at him!' he would emphatically announce, and this from a professional who took over 1,000 first-class wickets. There are many private demons lurking in the depths of even the best of cricketers.

Outside influences, real or imagined, can contribute to mental distress. By the same token, something in the brain can go awry and affect performance, even to the extent that full functioning out there in the middle becomes impossible. No one can continue to bowl with a pulled hamstring. No one can go out to bat if he has spent sleepless hours groping blindly about in the long dark night of the soul. The mind is subject to a number of disorders as much as the body is prone to an array of injuries. In the same way that not one body, in shape or function, resembles another, so one brain is unique and cannot be measured against another.

All that I can do, or try to do, is to chronicle the individual stories of cricketers – some well-known figures in the game – who have been willing to unburden themselves publicly of their private anguish, in the hope (theirs as well as mine) that their stories might encourage others to seek help where help is needed.

Where to start? Or, better still, who to start? Not being of a particularly religious disposition, I surprise myself by first seeking a clerical perspective. Andrew Wingfield Digby is a Church of England priest and former first-class cricketer, having represented Oxford University, where he studied philosophy. Famously, he was appointed by Ted Dexter as chaplain to the England cricket team, a post which he held from 1991–2001. He spent a great deal of time with the team and went on tour with them overseas. When he was first introduced to the players by the captain, Graham Gooch, Ian Botham was lying on the masseur's table. 'Don't worry, Wingers – me and Lamby will sing in the choir,' was Botham's typical cheeky quip. 'It broke the ice,' Wingfield Digby later confessed.

In your role as chaplain to the team, a sort of father-confessor, Andrew, I guess, you must have had to deal with a whole range of personal and professional problems. 'I was certainly entrusted with many pastoral issues with the team, but actually never depression – injury, infidelity, booze, homesickness, anxiety about life after cricket,' he told me, 'but I don't recall anyone coming to me depressed.'

He then provided this shaft of humour, so typical of the man. 'The only person who got depressed was me watching them bat sometimes!'

Was the England dressing room at that time full of confident fellows with larger-than-life personalities, who laughed in the face of failure and defeat? Certainly, some of them were. One cannot imagine Ian Botham suffering agonies of self-doubt. But I guess there were others who were not so thick-skinned, sanguine and relentlessly upbeat. The era of opening up publicly to mental health issues had not yet arrived. To admit to personal anguish in the alpha male environment of elite sportsmen was still seen as a sign of weakness, which would inevitably, it was felt, be exploited shamelessly by the opposition. Wingfield Digby provided appreciated support for external problems but those afflicting the heart and mind remained buried.

If the spiritual pathway offered little context, how about the professional analysis? Jeremy Snape was himself a former professional cricketer, a very successful one, it has to be said. Between 1991 and 2008, he played variously for Northamptonshire, Gloucestershire and Leicestershire and represented England in several one-day internationals. But it was his career post-cricket that I felt might be relevant to the subject of this book. He took a degree in sport psychology and founded Sporting Edge, which solves, or attempts to solve, business and sporting challenges. His regular podcasts, *Mind of Champions*, in which he interviews elite sportsmen and women, is very popular and well-regarded. He too has bent a questioning mind to the problems of mental health, most notably in the game which he knows the best.

'Is cricket the problem,' he mused aloud when I spoke to him, 'or are cricketers the first to speak out?' He was at pains to point out that the Professional Cricketers' Association (PCA) have been proactive in this regard, providing support and counsel for players and families. 'Players are now more comfortable talking about their mental issues,' he assured me. The demands of the game put enormous pressure on players, more so probably than other sports, he believes. They are away from home for long periods of time, separated from the support of family and friends, and hotel rooms can be very lonely places.

In his talks and podcasts, Snape stresses the importance of mental as much as physical fitness. Cut out the noise, he advises, have a business plan, set goals, focus fiercely. Motivation is all-important. Surround yourself with level-headed mentors. Put up a wall against negative influence. To lose a match when you have been beaten fair and square can be dealt with. But a worse loss is when you have not had the courage to fight. Cricket is a test of character. That is why they are called 'Tests'. When you have failed, you have to be honest and self-critical. Don't let yourself stew – *learn* from the experience.

My goodness, Jeremy, sports psychology has come a long way from when I was playing. We had nobody, no help or guidance whatsoever. You sank or you swam by your own endeavours.

Cricket is a team game, Snape reminded me, but the individual scrutiny is intense. The data to hand, itemising success or failure, is all too conspicuous and can be unbearable at times. That I had deduced from personal experience and from listening to former players. But then Snape added an extra dimension to the subject, one that I had hardly considered, not being a child of the technological revolution. 'Social media adds a further complex layer to the problem,' he said. 'Periods of relaxation after the day's play seems to have gone by the board. Now, you can be criticised on social media almost before you've taken your pads off, back in the dressing room. Millions of people can get stuck in at the press of a button and some of it is undoubtedly injurious and hurtful.' When I was playing at Hampshire, you might get criticised by *The Daily Telegraph* cricket correspondent the next day in his report of the game (and I frequently was), or you might choose not to read it and concentrate on Page 3 of *The Sun*. But your team-mates would take delight in reading out loud the relevant passage of the report, chronicling your incompetence. You had to laugh; there was no other way. 'Statistical scrutiny is now relentless,' Snape continued, 'and players today have to insulate themselves from constant judgement, much of it negative. Players must be instructed in self-awareness and be given lots of support.'

There is a further obstacle to work through, Snape identified, another set of rapids to negotiate as the turbulent stream of the mind rushes down to the sea. 'The pandemic has had an incalculable effect on the mental health of the population and cricketers, forced to operate in secure bubbles – not even allowed to sit with each other at meal-times …' He tailed off but the point had been well made. I cannot imagine going on a cricket tour and not being able to mix with, and enjoy, the company of team-mates, let alone not getting out there and savouring the ambiance and character of the country you are visiting. I was back at Hampshire recently for a former players' reunion. The new Rose Bowl is indeed a magnificent stadium, and it has proved popular with touring teams, not least because the Hilton Hotel overlooks the ground. No need for buses to transport team and support staff to and from the ground; everything is on site. During the pandemic, it hosted the Test match between England and West Indies behind

Albert Trott *uniquely played for two countries, Australia in 1895 and England in 1899. He was generally acknowledged as the finest all-rounder of his day but after 1900 his performances decreased as his weight ballooned. Unable to settle to anything after retirement, he shot himself in 1914.*

Andrew Stoddart *has the unique distinction of captaining England in cricket, rugby and Australian Rules football. A man of great zest for life but after retirement from cricket, he found working in the London Stock Exchange less stimulating and depressed by illness and burdened by debt, he shot himself in 1915.*

Harold Gimblett *was a hugely popular player for Somerset, both before and after World War Two,, renowned for his big hitting (265 sixes in his career). After cricket, he drifted, seemingly falling out with all his employers, unable to reconcile his former fame with his reduced circumstances. In 1978, he took his own life by ingesting an overdose of prescription drugs.*

Had it not been for Bradman, ***Wally Hammond*** *would have had every reason to stake a claim as the finest batsman in the world between the wars. A sad, sullen, uncommunicative man, he was not liked by both team-mates and opponents, who found his snobbishness and silences irksome. He had problems with his health, the primitive treatment and its after-effects of which undoubtedly contributed to his dark moods and clinical depression.*

***Jack Iverson**, with his unique finger spin, as if flicking away the stub of a cigarette, for a brief period in 1950/51 perplexed the England tourists in Australia, taking 21 wickets in the series. In later years, he suffered recurring bouts of depression and shot himself, aged 58, in 1973.*

***Stuart Leary**, pictured walking out to bat for Kent with Colin Cowdrey, also played football for Charlton Athletic. He had a long and successful career for Kent between 1951 and 1971. He took the cable car to the top of Table Mountain in Cape Town in 1988 and flung himself off. His body was not found until two days later.*

David Bairstow *played in four Tests and for Yorkshire throughout his long career, never giving of less than his best as an ebullient and energetic wicket-keeper. Following retirement, he suffered from depression and hanged himself at his home in 1998, aged 46.*

Peter Roebuck *was the strangest man I ever played cricket against. Highly academic, he graduated with a first-class degree in law at Cambridge University. But it was to first-class cricket for Somerset that he was drawn. As a player and captain, he felt secure in his gilded cage, in control of his life, but post-retirement was marred by scandal and court cases. On the point of being arrested in 2011 – for the second time in his troubled life – he flung himself from the sixth floor of his hotel in Cape Town, dying instantly.*

Once South Africa had been isolated from world cricket in 1968 because of its government's apartheid policies, the genius that was **Barry Richards** *was forced to tread the boards in local repertory while his team-mates, Gordon Greenidge and Andy Roberts, could trip the light fantastic in the West End. Those of us who were his team-mates were saddened by his woebegone countenance and depressed mood as the realisation sank in that he would never be able to showcase his talents on the world stage.*

Marcus Trescothick*, accompanied by his wife, Holly, attending the British Book Awards in 2009 where he was awarded the William Hill Sports Book of the Year, for his searingly honest account of his struggles with depression in* Coming Back to Me, *the book that started it all off.*

***Jonathan Trott** was the rock around which so many England innings were built between 2009 and 2015. His shock return from the Ashes series in Australia in 2013/14, citing 'stress-related illness', fooled no one. Depression had held him in an increasingly tight grip.*

***Graeme Fowler** made his name by scoring 201 in a nine-hour innings for England against India in Madras on the tour of that country in 1984/85. A year later, he could barely score a run and was discarded by England and found himself in the Lancashire second XI. He has been open about his depression since finishing with cricket and has contributed generously to this book.*

***John Barclay** had a successful career for Sussex between 1970 and 1986, captaining them for the last six years. He too has been open about his battles with depression and was another who contributed generously to this book.*

To the great surprise of his English teacher (me), ***David Nash*** *wrote a book,* Bails and Boardrooms *after his retirement from Middlesex, for whom he played from 1995–2009, chronicling his depression whilst a regular county player. He has been unstinting in his time helping me with this book. Incidentally, here he is being congratulated on an innings by my nephew, Tim Murtagh.*

*In 2004, **Steve Harmison** was rated as the No.1 bowler in world cricket. On the Ashes tour of Australia in 2006/07, he bowled the first ball of the series straight to a surprised second slip. Throughout his career, he hid his depression behind homesickness but since retirement, he has been more honest with his struggles.*

*Nobody could imagine the larger-than-life figure of England's star all-rounder, **Andrew Flintoff**, ever suffering from low self-esteem and depression. But that was his hidden battle, one that he has only really faced up to after he stopped playing.*

closed doors. The teams were strictly isolated from each other and contact between team-mates was kept to the barest minimum. From our vantage point in the dining room in the Shane Warne stand, I looked across at the Hilton Hotel, with balconies overlooking play at the other end of the ground. I imagined I was playing. I had been dismissed for a duck. Later, after the close of play, I would have been forced to retire to my room, alone, to stare miserably out on to the pitch where I had played that dreadful shot. All evening and no doubt much of the night. That way madness lies. No wonder Ben Stokes – and he has not been alone – felt it necessary to take time out from the game.

Then Snape presented me with an arresting image, a metaphor that works on so many levels. 'Cricket is dominated by failure,' he said. 'It is a pressurised environment, which rises the more successful you become. In order to protect ourselves, we put on a mask.' In view of the pandemic that was raging at the time of our conversation (on Zoom, I hasten to add), the image of a mask seemed particularly apt. I hate the things. Only surgeons and bank robbers wear masks. For the rest of us, they present a barrier against normal social intercourse. In order to talk to one another, we must do it face-to-face. There is so much tacit understanding that is taking place with different facial expressions. You can hide behind a mask … and that is precisely Snape's point. The word 'mask' of course derives from old French 'masque', meaning to hide one's face. In Tudor times, a masque was an elaborate, festive, courtly entertainment, often with an allegorical message, glorifying the court or the aristocratic patron. At the end, the players would remove their masks to reveal their identities. One of them could be the king himself; you never knew.

Snape's point is that we all, in one form or another, adopt a public face, behind which we hide our private insecurities. None more so than cricketers. A run of bad form can be emotionally draining. Injury can be debilitating. Fear of failure can be intimidating. Professional cricketers play in front of thousands of spectators who do not know them. They only see their score and their bowling analysis. Criticism is immediate and often merciless. I remember dropping a catch in front of thousands of Lancastrians at Old Trafford and they never let me forget it every time I was posted on the boundary. You just have to block your ears to the noise and concentrate on the next ball. The mask I adopted was one of supreme indifference to their barracking, even though I really wanted the ground to open up and swallow me.

The mask that players most commonly adopt in the dressing room is banter. We hide behind a pretence that nothing is serious and that everything, even somebody else's discomfiture, is worthy of a joke. Most of us accept this for what it is (nothing personal, old chap, just having a bit of fun) and we learn to laugh at ourselves as much as we laugh at others. But I cringe, now I am older and possibly wiser, when I consider that maybe not everybody was as thick-skinned as the rest of us and possibly behind that forced smile, somebody was suffering.

The mask in the dressing room was never allowed to slip.

'How are you feeling? Fit to play?'

'I'm fine, skip. No niggles this morning. Fit as a butcher's dog.'

Liar! Your back is still sore.

'We'd like you to open this morning. Are you okay with that?'

'Of course, skip. Can't wait to get out there.'

The last thing I want to do is open with that nasty fast bowler in their side.

'Loosen up! You're on next over, from the Pavilion End.'

'Righty-o, skip – two slips and a gully, please.'

The Pavilion End! He's got to be joking. I hate bowling from that end.

'Sorry, mate – we've decided to leave you out for this match.'

'That's fine, skip – fully understood.'

That means that bastard has taken my place.

'Twelfers – bring my lunch up, will you?'

'Certainly, mate. Pudding too?'

What does he think I am – his personal servant?

'We'd like you to go back to the second XI for a few matches. To regain a bit of form and confidence.'

'Probably a good idea, skip. Good luck up at Scarborough.'

Is this the end? Does that mean I've blown my last chance? The cricket committee are probably already voting whether to give me the sack.

That mask, Snape contends, is not a healthy barrier.

Cricketers cannot admit to their captain that they are upset by a row they had with their wife last night and perhaps are not in the right frame of mind to play. Cricketers cannot admit to their coaches that they are worried about a flaw in their technique, which has shredded their confidence, such that they do not know where the next run is coming from. Cricketers cannot announce to all and sundry that their run-up has gone to pot, and they don't know if they can even be relied upon to pitch the ball on the cut strip. Cricketers might be carrying an injury. They might have been dropped but they still have to remain upbeat even if the emotional blow is crushing them. Who am I? That is the question, Snape argues, that all cricketers must answer with unswerving self-honesty. The mask must be removed, he says, as soon as the individual walks through his front door. 'Look in the mirror, not out of the window!' is one of Snape's straplines. We must confront our own vulnerabilities. More and more cricketers are admitting this, he believes, and that can only be a good thing. A massive first step is to be brave enough to ask for help, for today help is there.

This is all to the good and Snape pays full tribute to the PCA for its enlightened attitude to the mental health of its members, past and current players. 'A lot of good work is going on under the radar,' he says. Yet, there is much work still to be done. Clearly, this more sympathetic philosophy has come too late for some and there may well be others who still believe there is a residual stigma attached to mental illness and depression. That is why these stories, some of them distressing, about those who have agreed to open up to me for this book, might help remove this stigma.

'Let me embrace thee, sour adversity, for wise men say it is the wisest course.'

Henry VI, Part III by Shakespeare

These are the first words of King Henry as he wanders in the forest, deliberating how he is going to recover his lost kingdom from the Yorkists. First, he must confront his own failings. In effect, he has got to look at himself in the mirror, not out of the window, where he can see only defeat and ruination. Grown men have been known to blanch when faced with a hostile crowd at Headingley or Edgbaston. It doesn't get any easier, facing up to depression (King Henry VI, incidentally, suffered from depression, though it was not called that; he was said to have 'lost his mind') but perhaps greater transparency can help others to understand what we are going through.

Growing up in south London in the 1950s, I was aware of the existence of the notorious gunman, safe-breaker and jailbird, Foxy Fowler, but I doubt that Graeme Fowler, born in Accrington, would have heard of him. *So why the nickname, Graeme; how come you were known in cricket circles as Foxy Fowler?* 'It was Bob Willis who first called me that. In my first Test match, he introduced me to the lads in the dressing room as "Foxy" and the name stuck.' I played with and against Bob Willis and had ample experience of his deadpan sense of humour and as he, like me, grew up in Surrey, it is more than likely he too had heard of the serial escapee, after whom he had named Graeme.

It is not the vulpine connotation of his nickname that drew me to Graeme Fowler but his public acknowledgement of his battles with depression. Would he be willing to share his experiences and talk about what had happened to him? He would indeed. He was more than willing; he sees it almost as his bounden duty to open up in the hope that greater transparency will help to remove the stigma that still attaches itself to mental ill-health.

Before we go any further, it is as well to remind ourselves of the rare talent that was Graeme Fowler that flashed across the English cricket firmament, burning brightly before being extinguished all too soon. He made his first-class debut for Lancashire as an opening batsman in 1979 and it was as an opener that he was picked for his first Test against Pakistan at Headingley in 1982. It was unkindly suggested at the time that he only owed his selection to the fact that 16 England players, including opening batsman Graham Gooch, had been banned for going on the rebel tour of South Africa. Fowler vigorously disputes this. 'I was scoring plenty of runs at the time. I deserved my place.' He scored 86 in the second innings and made his first Test hundred against New Zealand at the Oval in 1983. His second hundred – arguably his best – was against the fearsome West Indies pace attack at Lord's in 1984. When he reached his hundred, he happened to be batting with Ian Botham – later to become a lifelong buddy – who shook his hand warmly. 'Then, when the applause had died down a bit,' he said, 'Clive Lloyd, the West Indies captain and of course my Lancashire teammate, made a point of publicly shaking my hand too. I really appreciated that.'

However, it was Fowler's heroics in India the following winter that ushered him firmly into the international spotlight. In the fourth Test match of the series in Madras, in reply to India's first innings of 272, England amassed a total of 652 before declaring with seven wickets down. They owed this score to two men; Fowler made 201 and Mike Gatting 207. 'Me and Gatt kept each other going,' Fowler told me. 'After each over we would meet in the middle for a chat. At the end of the day, I was 149 not out, and I was knackered.' The next morning when Fowler reached his double hundred – the first by an Englishman in India – he remembers thinking, 'At least they cannot take this away from me.' He was out for 201 and three hours later, Gatting joined him as the second English double centurion in India. England won the match by nine wickets. The fifth Test in Kanpur was drawn, Fowler scoring 69 in his only innings.

That was his final Test: at the age of 27, he was never to play for England again. The British cricketing public – myself included – blithely assumed that when the ban on the 16 rebels had been lifted the following summer,

Fowler was cast aside by the selectors in favour of the vastly more experienced Graham Gooch. Disenchanted with this rejection, Fowler lost heart and form, unable to buy a run for Lancashire, eventually finding himself banished to the second XI. 'That was an unfair assumption,' he told me. 'After all, they still needed someone to partner Gooch, and I was the one in form and in possession of one of the opening slots.' No, the reason for his losing his place had a much more distressing source.

'When I came back from India,' he said, 'I was in great pain in my shoulder. The doctors didn't seem able to pin down the cause.' Eventually, he was asked if there had been any historical injury that might be affecting him. Then he remembered. Five years previously, he had been involved in a car accident, which had left him with a broken leg. Accident and Emergency had of course x-rayed his leg but had omitted to carry out any further investigation. Had they done so, they would have discovered that he had crushed two bones in his neck. 'So, effectively, I had been playing for five years with a broken neck.' He had been aware of a niggling pain in his neck, but had put it down to a trapped nerve or something. He had simply ignored it, made compensation in the way he moved and simply got on with the business of playing, the way professionals do. It's their job.

He told no one. Not the England management. Not the Lancashire captain. Not even his room-mate, Paul Allott. 'That was a bad decision,' he admitted ruefully. His performances for Lancashire nose-dived to the extent that he was dropped to the second XI. Still, he couldn't score a run. *No wonder you became depressed.* 'No, no!' he assured me, 'I was in a bad state emotionally, obviously. Who wouldn't be in a situation like that, one minute playing for England, the next playing in the county second XI? No, my depression, as we understand the condition, came later.' At the conclusion of a miserable season, he agreed to undergo treatment – physiotherapy, traction and then an operation. It was a success. 'When I came round,' he said, 'it was as if a light bulb in my body had been switched on. I was pain-free, with full movement restored.'

He was able to resume playing for his county career the following season and had what can genuinely be regarded as a successful first-class career. His England days were behind him, but he harbours few regrets. 'At least I still had a career,' he pointed out, 'and I did get that double hundred.' If you look at his Test career (21 caps, over 1,300 runs at an average of 35.32), you wonder why he was never recalled to the colours. Forget not that he opened the batting against West Indian fast bowlers of the calibre of Malcolm Marshall, Michael Holding, Joel Garner and Eldine Baptiste and against the Australian pair of Dennis Lillee and Jeff Thomson and still had a very respectable record.

A Lancashire opening batsman of an earlier era was Cyril Washbrook, who shared a successful opening partnership for England with Len Hutton for a number of years. He was publicly feted as an adventurous Test opener and revered in his native Lancashire, for whom he scored over 34,000 runs. However, once retired and now chairman of the cricket committee at Lancashire and latterly as president, he adopted a martinet style of governing, aloof and forbidding, with little understanding of how times and mores had changed. Few of the Lancashire players liked him. Graeme Fowler was no exception; it was inevitable that the individualistic streak in his make-up would clash with the ultra-conservative, reactionary committee man. Players of that era still talk of the essentially feudal conditions under which they were employed. 'The atmosphere in the Lancashire dressing room at that time was not great,' Fowler recalled. 'We had a non-playing captain, David Hughes. Well, he did play, but he didn't bat and hardly bowled, thus taking up a place in the side that could have gone to somebody that could do a job.'

In 1992, Lancashire had a wholesale clear-out of their playing staff. Alan Ormrod, Paul Allott and Graeme Fowler were summarily dismissed. 'I was told to clear my locker and leave immediately,' Fowler recalled, the bitterness still evident in his voice. 'I know of nobody in that era who left the club on good terms – David Lloyd, Clive Lloyd, John Abrahams, Peter Lee, me, Allott, Ormrod. Yes, I'd be lying if I said it didn't hurt. The implication was that I was a disruptive influence and had been disloyal to the captain. What utter rubbish!' *And this was what triggered the depression?* No, he did not think that was the case.

In fact, he continued his first-class career, joining the fledgling county, Durham, together with several older players, Ian Botham, David Graveney, Phil Bainbridge, Simon Hughes and Wayne Larkins. With a steadily increasing number of home-grown players, Durham slowly established themselves as a viable county, eventually winning the Championship in 2008, a feat they repeated the following year and again in 2013. It is worth remembering that three long-established counties, Gloucestershire, Northamptonshire and Somerset, have never enjoyed that distinction.

Fowler had retired from the game by then. Retired from playing the game, that is; he was very much involved in running the Durham University Centre of Excellence. The decision to close down these nurseries of first-class, and indeed Test, cricketers (Andrew Strauss was their most famous alumnus, incidentally) was sad and misjudged in Fowler's opinion, 'a retrograde step'. *Which of all these misfortunes in your life do you ascribe as the source of your depression?* 'Actually, none. People talk of a mid-life crisis, usually in one's forties and fifties. Cricketers suffer theirs earlier, in their thirties, when they retire. Each of us has to work out how best to carry on with the rest of our lives. No, my depression came as a bolt from the blue. Nothing to do with cricket, or no longer playing cricket.' As he started to outline the course of his battle with the black dog, I began to wonder whether cricket, or his total immersion in cricket, did not have something to do with his torment.

'Is cricket to blame or does the game attract people who are prone to depression?' he asked, thinking aloud. 'Cricket is a game based on failure,' he continued and then made a point that was stark in its substance. Don Bradman finished his Test career with a batting average of 99.94, which means in effect he scored a hundred every time he went to the wicket. Of course, that is demonstrably untrue. There were times when he failed – precious few, it has to be said – but there were other times when he scored a double hundred, even a triple hundred, and there were also not-out innings. Thus, it is reckoned that The Don 'failed' two times out of three whenever he went to the wicket. If Bradman fails that often, what does it say about the rest of us mere mortals scrambling around in his shadow?

But Fowler had resigned himself to his truncated international career; he still loved playing for his native Lancashire and enjoyed the 'project' that was Durham's infancy. He also felt fulfilled in his role as coach at the Academy. 'I loved the Christmas holiday,' he said. 'Time to relax, unwind and enjoy the family. It was Christmas of

1999. I'd had a persistent cough and had been prescribed antibiotics. My wife Sarah told me that I ought to see the doctor. I was surprised. But I haven't finished the course of tablets, I insisted. "Graeme," she said, "you haven't said a word to any of us for weeks." She was right. I had been cooped up in the conservatory for four weeks, reading the *Land Rover* magazine. The same one, my kids pointed out!'

Was there any hint anything was wrong? Did you feel ill? 'I was 47 and as fit as a fiddle. Reality dawned as a complete shock. Looking back, I recognised I had become completely uncommunicative. Everything seemed hopeless, pointless, worthless.' That feeling of desolation certainly struck a chord with me. *Any suicidal thoughts?* 'Not specifically, no. But I certainly wished I was not alive.' Quite where the danger line is drawn in anybody's mental disintegration varies from individual to individual. The professionals deemed that I was a danger to myself and had me immediately admitted to hospital. Fortunately, Fowler understood he needed help and straightaway sought it.

The doctor had little trouble in diagnosing clinical depression and told him bluntly that the road ahead would be long and bumpy. He prescribed a course of medication. 'I still didn't speak for a further six weeks,' Fowler continued. 'The drugs weren't working. I felt useless.' As with my experience, the prescribing of drugs is not a precise science. There are so many different types on the market and no one person's susceptibility or resistance to chemical intervention is the same as another's; it is very much a case of trial and error. To explore a different drug regime, it was necessary to wean himself off the current dosage – it takes about two weeks for the effects to clear the system – before another combination of drugs could be administered. 'Look, imagine you are hiding in a tree,' my consultant explained to me. 'We cannot cut off the branch on which you are perched, or you will come crashing down to the ground. We have to ease you off that branch and gently set you off on another branch.' *Did the new regime work?* 'Well,' Fowler replied, 'it dulled the pain, but I still felt like a zombie. Let me give you an example. One of the kids asked me the answer to the multiplication of seven by eight ... and I couldn't do it!'

Slowly, painfully, he adopted a sort of *modus operandi*. He had to admit to his family that he was ill and if at any time they asked him how he was that day, he would truthfully give them a number from 1 to 20, in ascending order of normality. Coincidentally, I was given the same advice, the same stratagem, to bring order to the daily chaos of misery, except my table ran from 1 to 10. 'The worst I have been is 5,' he confessed, 'and the best is 16.' By that token, I should say he has done remarkably well. 'It serves a purpose for the family,' he said. 'At least they have a ready reckoner on the state of my mood.'

He was convinced that the problem was a chemical imbalance in the brain. Accordingly, he submitted to the drug regime but refused any of the talking counselling, known as Cognitive Behaviour Therapy (CBT). 'I've always been able to sort out my own problems,' he explained. 'I have my own mind and make my own decisions. That's the way I played and that's the way I've lived my life – self-reliant.' *Did the different drugs work?* He seemed unsure. I could understand that. It was a question I was frequently asked. How do I know if they work? If I stopped taking them, I might feel worse. He did say that perhaps they were having an effect. His brain stirred: that much he was willing to concede.

He took three months' sick leave. He then went back to work but found it a struggle. At the conclusion of the season, he had a total mental collapse. 'I couldn't understand why I wasn't coping. I knew I had a good life and much that I was thankful for. But somehow, I couldn't reach it.' With typical robustness of mind, he took himself off his medication – without telling anybody, always a dangerous thing to do, as all my doctors warned. 'I felt strong enough to cope,' he insisted. 'Look, it's like any ongoing disease. Once you have it, you have it. It's how you cope that counts.' *Are you coping?* He believes so. A bit like a recovering alcoholic, he explained. You know the warning signs and you have the coping mechanisms, the defensive strategies, to see you through the onrushing storm. As a batsman, you rely on a well-honed technique to grapple with a hostile spell of bowling (in his case, West Indian fast bowlers or Indian spinners) and once you have weathered the storm, you feel more confident to forge ahead.

On reflection, do you think there were any warning hints, what the psychiatrists call 'trigger signs', earlier in your life that a tsunami was heading your way? 'Well, at the end of the season, I would go home, lie on the sofa and watch videos for a week, totally isolating myself from the family. I thought it was just my way of recharging the batteries after a long, hard season.' *I've been told that finally retiring from county cricket is akin to a kind of death. You mourn the passing of your career.* 'In a way, for me it was as if I was mourning the passing of another season. It brings you that much closer to the inevitable moment when you walk off the field for the last time.'

Having confronted head-on the reality of his situation, he started to re-evaluate his own personality and ponder how much what he always considered his strength – his self-reliance and his determination to sort out his problems his own way – might possibly have *contributed* to his depression. 'You have to be mentally tough to play cricket at the highest level,' he said, 'but ducking bouncers and standing up to sledging and aggressive appealing – that is not the same as being mentally strong.' Therefore, he does not blame cricket for his mental illness. 'I loved the pressure. I *thrived* on it.' He made the distinction between the emotional roller coaster that a batsman faces on a daily basis, and mental ill-health. 'A run of low scores can play havoc with your mind,' he pointed out. He had no need to remind me. 'It's all-consuming, isn't it?'

But he hit the buffers ten years after he had retired, so it wasn't a catastrophic loss of form that had 'triggered' it. So why now? He was anxious to find out. He approached Mike Brearley for help and advice. He could not have lighted upon a better sounding board. He knew Brearley and had played against him many times. Like Fowler, Brearley was an England player, he knew of the particular pressures that come with representing your country … and he knew what it was like to be dropped. The man whom the Australian fast bowler, Rodney Hogg, said had 'a degree in people', has in fact many professional qualifications to his name. He is a registered psychotherapist and psychoanalyst and a member of the British Psychoanalytic Council. Anybody who can get inside Ian Botham's mind to inspire him to heroic deeds should find Graeme Fowler a doddle.

In fact, Fowler found his chats with Brearley very helpful. Slowly, gently, Brearley unpicked Fowler's childhood, adulthood and cricket career, and suggested possible answers – or, at least, contributory factors – to his collapse. 'My mother never saw the good in me,' Fowler confided. 'She never praised me for anything.' That lack of maternal acknowledgement, Brearley postulated, had a profound effect on Fowler's personality. It forced him to be strong, able to shift for himself, to stand on his own two feet. 'It taught me to be resilient,' Fowler said. 'If I got knocked down, I would pick myself up, dust myself down and go again. I was always able to find a solution to any problem that arose.' Except he couldn't, not always. 'And when I wasn't able to sort it out myself, that is when I sank into depression.' All this, explained plainly and simply by Brearley, made perfect sense to him. 'Brearley told me to walk away from situations I couldn't handle. I didn't have to play the strong man all the time.' He used a phrase much bandied about by counsellors and therapists – 'It's all right not to be all right.'

In our day, we both agreed, mental health was *never* discussed in our dressing rooms. It was never brought up privately, even between room-mates. You never admitted that you were sick with nerves, that you were afraid you would let the side down, that you prayed for rain, that you just couldn't face going out there, alone, to take guard and to be made a fool, that you wished the ground would open up and swallow you, that you were not sure you enjoyed playing anymore. You would simply take a deep breath and plunge forward. I can imagine the consternation, contempt, laughter even, if Graeme Fowler had admitted in that Lancashire dressing room at any stage that he was struggling. Strong men don't cry. But yes, they do.

'I played with three players who took their own lives,' Fowler pointed out. 'So, we have to change the mindset that bottling it all up is a sign of strength. David Bairstow just couldn't cope with life without cricket.' He also mentioned Mark Saxelby, who played for Nottinghamshire and

Durham, who killed himself at the age of 31 by ingesting weedkiller. Danny Kelleher, who played for Kent from 1985–91, took an overdose of barbiturates at the age of 29. More names to add to David Frith's catalogue of poor, tormented souls.

Graeme Fowler has put words, wise words, into deeds. He has written a book, *Absolutely Foxed*, an honest appraisal of his cricket career and his subsequent battles with depression. It is an absorbing read, not just from a cricket perspective, but because it gives a blow-by-blow account of his illness and how he has striven to cope with it. He did several stints on *Test Match Special*. He has been put to good use by the PCA, doing the rounds of the counties, giving seminars on mental illness, what are the warning signs and how best to combat it. He does work for mental health charities and is in much demand as an after-dinner speaker, when he takes the trouble to talk about his own issues with depression up there with all the cricket stories. 'The main thing is,' he assures me, 'to keep mentally active.' Hear hear! That is one reason that I am writing this book.

Does all this talk, putting money where your mouth is, help you? 'No, not really. Writing the book was a strain because it brought it all back. And doing the seminars is no cakewalk either, for the same reason. You put on your public face, don't you?'

Aha! The mask that Jeremy Snape talks about, the one that we don for other people, the one that we must remove when we step through our front door so that we know who we really are. Look in the mirror not out of the window. Then, and only then, can we confront our own vulnerabilities, understand that we need help and embrace the means to secure it.

Fowler believes that if his book and his talks help even just one person, then the disquiet it might provoke in him is worth it. *How are things now?* 'I am more aware of it, both in me and in others. I know the signs. I recognise the symptoms. Talking about it does help. But there are still some people in the Dark Ages, who think depression is a result of weakness. That is the perception that we must work to change.' He finds painting a huge benefit. Jack Russell, the former Gloucestershire and England wicketkeeper, now a respected painter, introduced him to it and encouraged him to learn. Such a success has Fowler made of his second career (sorry, third – he is of course a writer!), that he has set up his own website, which shows examples of his landscape, portrait and abstract interpretations on canvas. *Are you still in love with the game?* 'Well, I was, until they brought in the awful Hundred!'

On that, and much else, we can agree.

For all cricketers, sometimes form and enthusiasm drain away, and each day, driving to the ground, opening the door to the dressing room and getting changed amidst all the usual noise and banter of 11 players preparing for the day's play, can feel like a chore, or even worse, a mental struggle. In his more reflective moments, the sufferer might ask himself, where did it all go wrong? When he was growing up, he lived for the days when he was going to play cricket. When he was offered a contract to play professionally, it was all he ever wanted to do. And what pride he felt as he pulled on his county sweater and what a thrill it was to return to the pavilion with three figures to his name, raising his bat in salutation to the members who had risen to their feet in acclamation. And now, he would rather be anywhere else than stepping out on to a cricket field. Instead of excitement gripping his vitals, it is now dread.

I am reminded of my old team-mate, Barry Richards, as I write this. He was popularly regarded – and not just by us who played with him day in, day out, but also by opponents of any county or country – as the finest batsman of his era, perhaps of any era. Famously, Don Bradman selected him to open for his All-Time Greatest XI, giving one of his reasons, 'Barry Richards was one of the best players of the short ball, opener or otherwise, ever.' Many would have added that he was the best player of the full-length ball as well – ever. It was Richards's misfortune to be born a South African at a time when his country was ostracised in any sporting context by the rest of the world for its apartheid policies; he played in only four Tests before the ban was imposed (in which he averaged 72.57, by the way, second only to Bradman's average of 99.94).

Slowly, as South Africa's re-admittance to world cricket became a vanishing pipe dream, Richards lost his enthusiasm for the game. Condemned for the remainder of his career to tread the boards in provincial repertory whilst team-mates Gordon Greenidge and Andy Roberts were strutting their stuff in the West End, he became an increasingly isolated and unhappy figure, deeply embittered but bravely soldiering on. There was no alternative. The ruses he got up to in order not to play – the list of improbable injuries grew and grew – became almost laughable, but none of us wholly blamed him. He was clearly deeply depressed but too proud to admit it and to seek help. Perhaps the club could have been more understanding and granted him time off, away from the game, to regain his motivation. Perhaps, we, his team-mates, could have been more understanding instead of expecting him to score a hundred every time he went to the wicket and been less censorious when he carelessly gave his wicket away, getting bored by the lack of challenge in the bowling. When the news came through that all players who had signed up for Packer and World Series Cricket (he had been one of the first to put his name to a contract) had been banned from county cricket (a ban, incidentally, that was overturned by the High Court), Richards's delight knew no bounds, even if it grated with one or two in our dressing room.

It was all such a pity, a waste of a talent, a suppression of a genius, and his slowly darkening mood should have had alarm bells ringing. Life after cricket was not kind to him either. Loss continued to stalk him in his personal life – the suicide of his son and the death of his partner to breast cancer. He was once asked how he felt about the tragedy of not having an extended Test match career and answered, 'A tragedy is losing your son or losing your partner. Not playing Test cricket is a disappointment.' The years have lent him a certain acceptance of life's vicissitudes but the sight of him standing disconsolately at slip, alone with his thoughts, as Hampshire were playing in front of a handful of spectators on one or other of county cricket's outposts will remain with me forever. Depression was writ large all over that lonely, hunched figure.

My father in his later years said that it is only at the beginning of the new year that you realise your friends, one by one, have dropped off the perch. It is the same at the beginning of each new season; you realise that familiar faces are now missing. I am not suggesting that they have died (though a wrench from our beloved game can resemble something like a *petit mort*) but that retirement, dismissal, chronic injury or relocation to another county have thinned out the ranks in the regiment and been replaced by new recruits. That is the way of professional sport. There is little room for sentiment. *'Le roi est mort. Vive le roi!'*

At the commencement of the 1976 season, I looked around the counties for a sight of a familiar figure and a good friend. 'Where's Dudley?' I wanted to know. It was not until we played Surrey that I was able to enquire of his erstwhile team-mates of the whereabouts, and the reasons for the disappearance, of Dudley Owen-Thomas. We were exact contemporaries as schoolboys and had played together for Surrey second XI, before he went up to Cambridge University and I made my way to Hampshire via Southampton University, and our county careers diverged. Nonetheless, we remained on the most cordial of terms whenever our paths crossed and now, I wanted to know what had become of him. 'Cuddles? Oh, he's retired,' was all I got from his former team-mates. 'Cuddly Dudley' was his not altogether unkind nickname. Retired? I had never been so shocked in my life. Retired! When he seemingly had the cricket world at his feet. How come?

He had a prodigious record in schoolboy cricket, recognised officially in 1967 as the leading schoolboy all-rounder in the country (he bowled useful off-breaks to supplement his undoubted talents as a batsman). He went up to Cambridge to read law … and to play cricket. 'We had a bloody good side,' he reminded me, 'the equal of one or two of the counties.' This was no idle boast. The 1971 Cambridge side included: Majid Khan, captain (Pakistan and Glamorgan), Peter Johnson (Notts), Phil Edmonds (England and Middx), Mike Selvey (England and Middx), John Spencer (Sussex) as well as Owen-Thomas, who scored 146 in the 1971 Varsity Match, which so nearly secured victory (Oxford's last-wicket pair were grimly hanging on at the death) and 114 in the 1972 match that did secure a victory for his side, by an innings and 25 runs. By now, he had already made his debut for Surrey, and he played ten matches for the county after coming down that year, finishing the season with an average of 35.62. That same year, he was named as the Cricket Writers' Young Cricketer of the Year. A rosy future beckoned. Great things were expected.

'I was selected for the MCC tour of India, Pakistan and Sri Lanka that winter,' he told me. My jaw dropped. I had researched that tour extensively for my book on Tony Greig (when he truly announced himself on the world stage) and I know that Owen-Thomas was not one of the tourists. Patiently, he explained the extraordinary circumstances that swirled around the touring party even before they had quit these shores, a story that was not reported at the time and even now remains little-known by the general public, me included.

The incumbent captain of the England team was Ray Illingworth and the selectors fully expected him to lead the team in the subcontinent. However, almost at the 11th hour, he withdrew, citing inadequate financial remuneration provided by MCC as the reason. (Whenever did Illy *not* complain – often with some justification – about meagre pay for professional cricketers?) The selectors were left in a quandary. They spread their net far and wide for a replacement captain, there being no obvious candidate from within the ranks of the rest of the team, and eventually they lighted upon Tony Lewis, the Glamorgan captain, as yet uncapped by England. The trouble from Owen-Thomas's point of view was that Lewis was a batsman, as was Owen-Thomas. 'So, I was dropped from the party to make way for him,' was his glum conclusion.

In actual fact, Lewis, the only player to make his debut for England as captain, did a fine job on that tour and returned home with the reputation of MCC abroad fully restored. Illingworth was immediately restored to the captaincy in 1973 and Lewis only played in one more Test before retiring and concentrating on his broadcasting and journalistic career. Owen-Thomas? He was the forgotten man. Few even knew that he had originally been picked for the tour and summarily discarded before he had even been measured up for that iconic MCC blazer.

'It affected me deeply,' he admitted. 'Perhaps it should not have, but it did. Maybe I should have shrugged off the disappointment, scored lots of runs and forced the selectors to think again. But it didn't work out like that.' He reeled off from memory his averages in the three seasons following his disappointment: '1973 – 30.04, 1974 – 15.61, 1975 – 26.95. The deterioration was plain to see.' *Why?* 'I was depressed. I can see that now. I was no longer enjoying my cricket. I just had to get out.'

Was it loss of form that caused his depression or was the fact that he was depressed the cause of his loss of form? He is unsure of the answer. 'Perhaps it was a bit of both,' he concludes. Certainly, he was not happy at Surrey. Would he have thrived at another county, whose dressing room was not as unforgiving as Surrey's traditionally has always been? Maybe that is why the Brown Caps have over the years turned out to be serial winners; like Yorkshire, another historically successful county, it has been the school of hard knocks, of tough apprenticeships, that churned out hardened champions.

If you lose form, the dressing room can be a very lonely place. Owen-Thomas felt isolated; the harder he tried the worse it got. In the end, something had to give, if only to spare his sanity. It was John Edrich, not one noted for his sympathetic advice, who pointed to the pathway out of his misery. 'Look, Dudley,' he said, 'why scratch around making a pittance as a professional cricketer when you can make a fortune working as a lawyer?' At the conclusion of the 1975 season, Owen-Thomas informed Surrey he no longer wanted to play. He left the club and set about training for the legal profession. 'I wouldn't exactly say I made a fortune,' he laughed, 'but I managed to carve out a decent career in law.'

Maybe so. But what a pity he was not able to fulfil his rich, early promise, one of the most exciting young cricketers of his era. I, for one, believed he was destined for great things but circumstances, and possibly a temperament more given to introspection, accompanied by periods of self-doubt and desolate mood, decreed otherwise.

One morning, I received a telephone call from Lt. Col. J.R. Stephenson, assistant secretary of MCC. Normally, communication with the good colonel in order to arrange the annual fixture between the club and Malvern College was done by post. On this occasion, I was favoured with a personal call. They had a young lad at Lord's who was destined to be the future Middlesex wicketkeeper for many years, he told me, but he was naive and a bit raw. Would we, the College, be willing to take him on for a couple of years, in order that he might mature and maybe have a few rough edges smoothed away? The colonel's hand was bitten off and accordingly, David Nash presented himself at the beginning of the 1994 academic year at the front door of No. 7, where I was the housemaster, to have those rough edges duly evened out. I have to say in this regard I failed in my mission; from first to last, David remained an unreconstructed Cockney. Far from adopting the public-school drawl, his accent remained unashamedly north London. He started off by calling me 'mate'. When I explained to him that this was not altogether appropriate, he compromised by calling me 'mate, Sir'. Furthermore, I found it a frustrating battle to get him to do much work, but he survived academically because he had a native wit and a sharp intelligence. The fact was that he was adored by everybody, staff included, at the College because he was such a cheerful, friendly, buoyant sort of chap, with an entertaining sense of humour. Of course, his cricketing abilities were undeniable (he was a more than useful footballer too) and he helped raise the standard of our first XI to hitherto untold heights.

As predicted, he had a long and successful career at Middlesex, culminating in a rewarding benefit, largely because he had been as popular with the club members as he had been with Malvernians. He went into business following his retirement from cricket and to nobody's surprise, made a fortune. I have kept in touch with him; he was a faithful old boy of the school, regularly turning out for the Old Malvernians Vets football team, together with my two sons. He still calls me 'mate', though the 'Sir' has subsequently disappeared.

He then wrote a book, *Bails and Boardrooms*. This shocked me on two counts. Hitherto, he had betrayed not the slightest hint of any literary inclination, yet the book was undeniably written by him; he had obviously spurned the use of a ghost writer. But it was the content – specifically, those passages pertaining to his cricket career – that left me wide-eyed in astonishment. Within those pages is the distressing admission – contrary to all outward appearances – that he had not greatly enjoyed his time playing county cricket. In fact, there had been times that he positively hated playing; he would rather have been anywhere else other than out there in the middle. He writes: 'I dropped Martin Lowe of Durham live on Sky TV. I knew the game was up. I was mentally shot. Next over, I feigned injury and came off. That was the day that I was able to be honest with myself about the struggle that was to be the biggest of my life – my mental health. Cricket had destroyed it.'

Looking back, he recognised that the heavy veil of depression had been hanging over him for several years prior to his dropped catch on television. Even at school, at Malvern College, he had been having 'life or death moments', which would have shocked his friends, his teachers and even me, his housemaster. We had no intimations of his inner turmoil. Outwardly, he maintained the role of the 'cheekie chappie', full of bonhomie and good cheer. He was demonstrably superstitious and always followed a strict regimentation of quirks and obsessive ritual … but all wicketkeepers are a bit zany, I lazily told myself. Rather like goalkeepers, there is often an eccentric side to them. You only have to think of the repetitive tics and foibles, habits and repetitive mannerisms of John Murray, Alan Knott, Jack Russell and the like to understand what I mean. I just presumed David was a perfectionist and never wanted to upset the status quo that had served him well enough. For goodness' sake, don't change a thing; we don't want to tempt fate.

Well into his first-class career, by the age of 25, he thinks, he had developed serious mental issues 'as a result of playing cricket', he asserts confidently. 'I was good at the game,' he told me later, 'but I did not believe it was the real purpose in my life.' Good at the game he assuredly was but he was not enjoying it. He was perpetually anxious about his performances and, oddly, believed he was a better member of the Middlesex side *off* the pitch than on it. He was happiest when it rained and there was little, or no, chance of play. He started inventing excuses not to play, or to hand over the gloves or to be demoted down the batting order. It was Ed Joyce, the captain, who eventually called David out. He believed that his wicketkeeper was not pulling his weight and eventually dropped him from the side. David was furious, blaming Joyce for all his subsequent woes and the relationship between the two was fatally fractured. Yet, in his heart of hearts, David knew the truth of Joyce's criticisms, and slowly the realisation that his career had hit the buffers dawned on him as his replacement, Ben Cox, made a hundred and kept well. 'I loved the dressing room, the banter with the lads, the whole lifestyle of a professional cricketer but I had come to hate the game.'

In his book, Nash contemplates the loneliness of the player that makes cricket unique. He quotes an extraordinary observation by the late Bob Woolmer, Test cricketer and respected coach: 'Review the raw, split-second data of what happens when a batsman executes a shot, and you wonder how anybody survives more than one delivery.' Yet batsmen are expected to survive hundreds of deliveries and execute multiple shots in order to build up a decent score. The pressure is immense.

The dressing room at Middlesex, as it was with all counties, was a 'school of hard knocks', as Nash described it. He was 'called out' in front of the whole team and criticised publicly. He felt 'belittled', which ate away at his sense of self-worth. Inadequacy gnawed at him, and he began to dread even entering the dressing room, let alone going out into the middle to perform. Cricket had become a chore; what once had been enjoyable and fun had now chipped away at his mental equilibrium. This was a toxic frame of mind in which he found himself, but he felt powerless to do anything about it. He was desperately unhappy but hid his depression, put on a brave face and sought no help.

For there was no help to be had, he claimed. 'The game needs to foster an environment,' he said, 'in which players feel free to talk about their issues.' Understanding of the mental as well as the physical pressures to which cricketers in the first-class game are subjected was still in its infancy. He hopes that things are better these days, following several high-profile players coming clean in public about their experiences of depression, but he does not believe that the battle is won. 'I fear for the young lads today,' he said, 'and worry that they still do not get the support they need.'

Following his retirement from cricket, Nash set up his own business, determined that the mistakes in player welfare that he had experienced at Middlesex would not be repeated in his workforce. His depression and moments of despair in his playing career stemmed directly, he believes, from not feeling confident enough, because the environment discouraged it, to admit his vulnerabilities to his captain, team-mates and coaching staff. In his business, he advocates 'psychological safety', in which each team member feels safe to take reasonable risks and to feel confident enough to buy in to the 'one in, all in' ethos of the company. He has seen similar problems in the world of business as those he knew existed in the world of cricket, where the bosses have treated objectives and goals as separate from the well-being of their employers. 'Wrong! Wrong! Wrong!' he exclaims passionately. A happy workforce is more likely to go the extra mile because they feel emotionally invested in the company's fortunes.

It is a policy that has succeeded handsomely. His entrepreneurial skills have been put to the best possible use and his hospitality business is now a multi-million-pound enterprise. However, he has not forgotten his unhappiness as a cricketer. He has raised hundreds of thousands of pounds for charity and contributed generously to the initiatives set up by the Professional Cricketers' Association to protect players' mental welfare.

His last words to me … 'I have been in situations in cricket where there has been no safety net, and it's soul-destroying. I wouldn't wish my worst enemy to have to go through that.' In the same way that he charmed Malvern College, he was – and remains – among the most popular Middlesex players in living memory and his story has a happy ending. 'It's good to talk,' he emphasises, echoing that oft-repeated phrase beloved of counsellors and psychotherapists. Nash is a survivor. As I have expounded in these pages, not all cricketers similarly affected had such a fortunate outcome.

People often ask me about Robin Smith, who was a fellow Hampshire player, but regretfully our careers did not overlap, and I have never met him. But like all cricket lovers I followed his progress in the Hampshire team and thence into the England team, where his dynamic and forceful batsmanship, especially against the fearsome West Indies fast-bowling attack in the 1990s, won huge admiration, even amongst his opponents. It was whispered at the time that he was not so successful against the spinners, and it is undoubtedly true, as he himself freely admits, that Shane Warne got into his head and started to dominate him psychologically. As I have said in an earlier chapter, spin bowlers can scramble the mind just as much as a fast bowler, who are intent not so much on getting inside the head as knocking it off completely. If what Smith said of Warne is true, he would not have been the first to be so ensnared. For all these supposed weaknesses as a batsman, Smith's record in Test cricket stands up to scrutiny. He played in 62 Tests and finished with a batting average of 43.67, and this in an era when England were getting regularly hammered by the big boys, Australia and West Indies.

Whilst he was playing cricket, engaged in something he loved and was rather good at, something he was born to do, he was happy and felt fulfilled. He later admitted that he was not quite so self-confident as his public demeanour proclaimed – he had donned his mask for his audience – and nothing prepared Smith for the bleak landscape he stumbled upon when he retired. Perhaps that was part of the problem. There was no help, no guidance, no training from the authorities to prepare professional cricketers for life after the umpire has raised his finger for the last time. In his book, *The Judge* (that was his nickname at school, one that has stuck throughout his life, on account of his mop of hair, resembling a judge's wig, though in this case the title hints at an analogy of moral judgement), Smith writes, 'When the bubble bursts as a professional sportsman, if you haven't prepared for life after, you're in serious trouble.' Smith had not prepared for life after and he found himself right there.

He missed the banter and the camaraderie of the dressing room, the structure of the daily life of a professional cricketer and no doubt the acclamation of the cheering crowd after a fine innings. Cricket was what defined him; now he was just a former cricketer, and the world is full of them. He drifted, becoming a bit of a recluse. Nothing replaced the smell of the greasepaint and the roar of the crowd, to quote the title of a Broadway hit. He felt isolated, worthless, 'weary, stale, flat and unprofitable', as Hamlet said. He took solace in alcohol, draining a bottle of vodka in one go. One day, he picked up his daughter from school and, drunk as he was, he drove over the kerb. Frightened, she asked to get out. Later he was hauled over by the police and breathalysed. For a second, the cop paused and blinked as he read the dial. Apparently if the alcohol in your blood stream registers 0.3, you should be unconscious. If it is 0.4, you will be in a coma. Any higher and you would likely be departing this life. Smith's reading was 0.4. Undeniably, he was in a bad way.

His life was rapidly falling apart. Various businesses had failed, he was running up large debts, his wife had left him, his daughter was ashamed of him, and the dark mantle of depression had wrapped itself around his world. 'I was sitting on the beach in Perth, with the Rendezvous Hotel behind me, thinking how was I going to end my life … I knew I was going to commit suicide but I didn't know what day it would be or how I was going to do it.'

He stepped back from the brink, he recounts, when he witnessed a shocking suicide first-hand. A woman jumped to her death from the very apartment block where he was living. That could have been me, he reflected, and there and then, he resolved to clean up his act. With the help of his brother Chris, a fellow Hampshire man and England cricketer – who has always been there for him and always tried to help, but now he was ready to be helped – he dried out, got himself a job and put his life back together again.

Despite the positive note on which he ends the book, word on the grapevine is that Smith is not totally free of the black dog. Like most depressives, the struggle is a daily one. As a fellow sufferer once said to me, 'You have to be on your guard. You might think you are out of the woods but there is always another forest over the horizon.'

Here is another story that caught everybody by surprise. It is a crying shame that a doughty servant of England cricket, who played 63 Tests for his country and took 226 wickets – bowling fast – should be remembered for one ball, quite possibly the worst ball bowled in an international match. It was the first ball of an Ashes series, and it was bowled at Brisbane in the opening Test of the 2006/07 series. Steve Harmison, one of the heroes of that unforgettable Ashes summer of 2005, marked out his run, wiped his brow with the sleeve of his shirt, bounded in to the left-handed Justin Langer and let go … The ball went straight into the surprised hands of his captain, Andrew Flintoff, fielding at second slip.

Somehow, you knew that the tone of the series had been set by that one wide. How can a five-match series be settled by one ball, not the last but the first? Ridiculous. The second ball could have been a wicket. A lot can happen over the course of five Test matches. Yet, to nobody's surprise, England were walloped 5-0, all five victories for the Australians coming by huge margins. It was the worst hammering England had suffered in Australia since J.W.H.T. Douglas led his side to an equally embarrassing 5-0 whitewash in 1920/21.

I said it was a crying shame and that was not just a figure of speech. The effect on Harmison's self-confidence and mental well-being was profound. After the dust had settled, he said later back home, 'From the very first ball of that series, I hated the game of cricket … I can't think of a worse ball to bowl than that. I can't remember ever bowling a worse ball than that.' How had it come to this? He had gone from being the number one bowler in the world (according to the ranking statistics) in 2004 to bowling a series-defining wide at Brisbane in 2006. 'I'd gone from feeling on top of the world to being in a clinic in the Priory,' he wrote in his book, *Speed Demons*. In point of fact, his battles with depression had started well before that fateful delivery. He believes these feelings, which sometimes led to thoughts of suicide, had always afflicted him.

It was well known among his friends and team-mates that he suffered from homesickness and hated touring. In his book, he takes us back to his greatest triumph with a ball in his hand, his 7-12 against the West Indies in Kingston, Jamaica, in December 2004. He found it hard to celebrate. He had been away from his family for ten weeks and wanted nothing more than to come home. 'It's just being away that kills me,' he said. But it was more than just homesickness that was the problem. Even during the summer of 2005 – the Greatest Ever Ashes Series, as it was dubbed – 'the horrible truth was that these same feelings that had consumed me on trips abroad were overpowering me again – and this time it had nothing to do with being away from home.'

Seeking medical advice, he admitted to contemplating driving his car into another in order to get out of touring South Africa in 2004/05. People never took him seriously, he contended, calling it 'homesickness', until Marcus Trescothick shone a merciless light upon the problem. He never admitted as much to the England management for fear he would be ostracised and dropped permanently from the team.

It was not until he was admitted to the Priory, when a proper diagnosis was made and medication prescribed, that he realised the extent and severity of the problem. The relief at finally getting it off his chest was immeasurable. He said that he drank heavily on occasions, but alcohol was not the cause. 'It just filled a void … but I was a thousand times worse the next day … it was clear I was clinically depressed, and medication would be the way forward. I've been on it ever since … I can't say there haven't been dark times where I have thought it would be easier if I wasn't here.'

Thankfully he is still here and though he wishes he had opened up earlier about his mental struggles, when he was playing and hiding behind the shield of 'homesickness', his searing honesty has subsequently added to the swelling chorus that demands our cricket authorities recognise before it is too late that cricket is a strange game and its players peculiarly susceptible to what he called 'our demons'.

Jonathan Trott, a native South African, was for several years the mainstay of England's batting, projecting an aura of permanence, not least with his interminable scratching of his mark at the crease between balls. Like many of his team-mates of that era, he can point to the Ashes success of 2010/11 as the highlight of his career, but it is a sad fact that he will probably be better remembered for abandoning England's tour of Australia of 2013/14 immediately after the first Test in Brisbane, citing stress and anxiety and a need for a complete break from the game. The occasion and the circumstances surrounding his 'breakdown', as he called it, are unflinchingly detailed in his autobiography, *Unguarded*, which I have read, and which provides much food for thought in my examination of mental illness within the context of the game of cricket.

Much of what Trott describes sounds achingly familiar, even though he is adamant that his troubles were anxiety-related and not the result *per se* of depression. Doctors, psychiatrists, psychologists and counsellors may disagree on the actual wording of their diagnosis but the manner in which Trott's symptoms presented themselves are recognisable to all who have been similarly afflicted.

In describing what was going through his mind during that Test match in Brisbane before returning home to

England, the pain he was experiencing is raw and sharp: 'I felt I was being led out to face the firing squad by the time we reached Brisbane. I was a condemned man. Helpless, blindfolded and handcuffed. Mitchell Johnson was to be my executioner.'

Johnson, the Australian fast bowler, Mitchell Johnson, had become Trott's nemesis. Trott had faced all the fast bowlers around the world and been thoroughly examined – as any Test batsman is – by the short ball. Indeed, batting at No. 3, he would have been exposed to more than the odd bouncer, but he had always coped. All of a sudden he felt he could no longer cope. His nerve, together with his technique, had deserted him. The disturbance of his mind is vividly detailed: 'Struggling with the short ball isn't the same as any other problem in cricket. If you are struggling on off stump, people talk about your technique. If you are struggling with the short ball, they talk about your courage. I felt I was being questioned as a man. I felt my dignity was being stripped away with every short ball I ducked or parried. It was degrading. It was agony.'

But it wasn't cowardice at all. His problems, not just with a bat in his hand, had been bubbling away below the surface for some time. Mitchell Johnson was the agent which brought the mixture to the boil. Kevin Pietersen, Trott's team-mate in the England side, had noticed something was amiss with his friend and fellow South African even before Johnson had marked out his run-up: 'He doubted himself and even seemed to be disgusted with himself. You could see he was questioning what sort of man he was. He was a proud, strong man and all of a sudden, he was sitting in the corner of the dressing room crying. It was horrible to watch. Horrible.'

I well recall the words of my psychiatric consultant in one of our sessions who remembered I was an English teacher and thus referred me to Charles Dickens and his novel *A Tale of Two Cities*, and the words of Sydney Carton: 'Heaven knows we need never be ashamed of our tears, for they are the rain upon the blinding dust of earth, overlying our hard hearts.' Trott felt shame at his weakness but nobody, even the alpha-male Kevin Pietersen, blamed him. Clearly, Trott's world was imploding. He didn't know why, he didn't know what to do or how to seek help; he simply did not want to be there. This is what bewildered him. All he had ever wanted to do was to play cricket. He was now a successful and respected member of the England team; his boyhood dream had been realised. He had pitted himself against the best and risen to the challenge. Now, he was reduced to an empty shell, barely able to put one foot in front of the other, let alone face a left-arm quick bowler on one of the fastest and bounciest wickets in the world.

His predicament meant only one course of action was possible, that he abandon the tour and return home. The official line was that he was suffering from a 'stress-related illness'. When I read that in the newspapers, I thought to myself, he has depression, the poor lad; the signs are obvious. He maintained at the time – and still does – that it was not depression that precipitated the breakdown but stress, anxiety and burn-out. I would contend that all these obvious root causes are interlinked. The stress of facing bowling in excess of 90mph, with the accompanying risk of serious injury, the demands that it places upon your courage and technique, are peculiar to an international cricketer. The anxiety, the fear of failure is of course common to all sportsmen and women, but the relentless schedule imposed on any first-class cricketer, day in, day out, week in, week out, for months on end, with no break, is not. Cricket is a long game and the opportunities for respite few and far between. Trott wouldn't be the first Test cricketer who felt that he needed to step off the treadmill for a while, to save his sanity.

Trott believed that a rest and a break from cricket would do the trick and that he would soon be back in the fray. He was wrong. A premature return to county cricket with Warwickshire brought it home to him that he was still in a mess. He lacked energy, enthusiasm, joy, his self-confidence had been shot to pieces, and he was lost, mentally bereft. The future looked bleak.

He sought the help of a sports psychiatrist who diagnosed what he called 'situation-based anxiety', a term that Trott felt comfortable with. Once you know what is wrong with you and that you are definitely not going mad, once you have a tag to attach to your unhappiness, all at once doesn't seem so dark. Trott felt his mood lift. He started playing again. England wanted him back in the team. He was selected to go on the tour of the West Indies in 2015. It did not work out well.

Perhaps he should not have gone. Perhaps he should have been more honest with himself, or at least looked at himself with a more critical eye. Perhaps he lacked sensible, cool-headed advice. Andrew Strauss, the England captain, later went on record to say, 'I didn't think there was any way back for him after Brisbane, to be honest.' Yet Strauss has the utmost admiration for the man in attempting a comeback like that. 'To fight his way back into contention was incredible. He had to dig so deep to do so; he had to challenge himself in ways that he had never challenged himself before.'

Brave, no doubt, but perhaps it wasn't wise? The brain is not like other parts of the body. The healing process is long, arduous … and unpredictable. In Trott's own words: 'It took one ball in Antigua. One ball on my return to Test cricket for me to realise my return wasn't going to work out. One ball to realise there would be no fairy-tale ending.'

At the end of the tour, which had indeed not gone well for him personally, as he knew it wouldn't, he announced his retirement from international cricket. 'As I got back into the dressing room that last time, I remember thinking, "Thank God that's over."'

My memory stirred when I read that. It was Harold Gimblett, 'the tormented genius of cricket', who also had said, 'Thank goodness that's over!' when news came through that he had been dropped from the England side after only two Tests.

It seems harsh to remember Trott solely for his abandonment of an Ashes tour almost before it had begun, no matter how highly he is regarded for his courage in attempting to make a comeback and for his searing honesty in his book. Let us not forget – he hasn't – that he played in *two* Test matches in Brisbane. In the first on the 2010/11 tour, he scored 135*, helping England to come back from the dead to secure a famous draw, from which they won the series. In his Test match career, he scored near enough 4,000 runs in 52 matches at a very respectable average of 44.08. Some of those runs were eked out when he was far from well. He questioned his courage; his team-mates never did. He can feel proud of what he achieved, not least for opening up publicly about his mental struggles. One of the last sentences in his book says it all: 'The game spares no one.'

All-rounders are a breed apart. They seem to play their cricket with an exuberance of spirit and a gaiety of heart. Not for them the pressure to perform and the anxiety of failure. If they get a duck, they can always bowl an inspiring spell later in the day. If their bowling is carted all around the park, they more than likely will dazzle with the bat when their turn comes. The clue to their balanced temperament and breezy nonchalance possibly lies in the name. 'All-rounder' suggests a personality that is versatile, resourceful, well-grounded, clear-sighted. That is why the mental struggles of two of England's finest all-rounders since the war, Andrew Flintoff and Ben Stokes, once the public became aware, came as such a shock. Both gave every appearance of indestructibility, steel-plated in their feats of derring-do. But, as we have seen so often in the case studies outlined in these pages, 'where the waters ran smooth, he found it deepest', as the fable goes.

Since retirement from cricket, Flintoff has carved out for himself a successful and lucrative career presenting television shows on various subjects. In one of them, *Freddie Flintoff: Hidden Side of Sport*, he talks candidly with guests about the serious effects of depression. He spoke about his own personal problems when he was captain of England at a time when they were playing badly, and his position was coming under increasing fire from the media and public. He was undoubtedly depressed and said that the stigma attached to the illness prevented him from ever admitting to it whilst playing. He hid it under a cloak of bravado, high jinks, hearty bonhomie and bouts of heavy drinking. Remember the incident when he had to be helped from the choppy waters of the Caribbean Sea, having fallen from a pedalo following an eight-hour drinking session? He cultivated an image of indestructibility but underneath he was suffering torments of self-doubt.

Following the Ashes defeat in the 2006/07 series, he found himself weeping uncontrollably. He was the England captain yet he 'didn't want to get out of bed, never mind face people'. It was not just the onerous responsibilities of captaining his country – and losing the Ashes – that brought it on; he had been suffering for years but chosen to 'suffer in silence'. He says it helps talking to people about it and that 'I'm on medication and I now know how to deal with it'. Looking back on his career, he said, 'As a sportsman, you build a certain persona. In my case it was unflappable, fun-loving Freddie. The public look at you and think you don't have a care in the world.'

It would appear that, on the contrary, Flintoff had all the cares in the world but sadly for him, while he was playing, nobody knew.

In 2021, when Ben Stokes took 'an indefinite break from cricket to protect his mental health', as the ECB communique put it, the surprise was even greater. By all appearances and in view of his heroics with bat and ball, he had put behind him that brawl outside a nightclub in Bristol which led to him being charged (but later acquitted) with affray. Surprise soon gave way to sympathy. In the not-so-distant past, the news would have been met with expressions of incredulity, even scorn; you could have heard in your mind's ear, the uncompromising words of censure from former professionals on the lines of 'It were 'arder in our day, an' we were paid peanuts too, not like the pampered millionaires these days.'

Perhaps times *have* changed. Maybe people are beginning to appreciate that the pressures of modern life do take a toll on international cricketers, notwithstanding the greater financial rewards on offer. And none can remain unsympathetic to the particular strains of living in a bio-secure bubble during the pandemic. Yes, we all had to exist as best we could during lockdown, but few had to perform on the field of play at the same time, in front of deserted stands, and condemned to solitary confinement in a hotel room once stumps had been drawn. Furthermore, Stokes had to deal with the death of his beloved father, who had been suffering from a brain tumour in the last year of his life. Stokes has openly criticised the ECB for not allowing him more time to spend with his father. He later admitted that he was never sure that he would ever play again during those dark days.

But emerge he did from his self-imposed detachment to the captaincy of his country and to even greater success and acclaim. To his great credit, he has been quite open about his mental health issues. 'There's always a negative feeling around mental health,' he said, 'but I took my break and spoke to someone, and I will continue to do that.' That can be a qualified psychotherapist or counsellor or trusted confidant, all better sounding boards than the echo chamber of your own mind. 'I don't want anyone to feel the way I did,' he continued, reiterating the wish of so many sufferers, 'because I wasn't in a good place and I'm not afraid to admit it. I was in a dark place and having some very difficult thoughts.'

But it was not always so. Joe Root, a team-mate in the England side and a close friend, spoke about his surprise when Stokes opened up publicly about his mental struggles. He didn't know – none of the team knew – even though it was perceived as a close-knit group in that dressing room. 'I think it shows great courage, great bravery,' said Root, 'to come out and speak openly about that stuff and some of the struggles he has been through.' Root believes that the game has come a long way in helping players cope with mental issues since the start of his career, naming Marcus Trescothick and Jonathan Trott as leaders who have blazed a trail through the thickets of ignorance and intolerance.

Chapter 8

Marcus Trescothick

'As I placed the navy-blue cap with the three lions in my bag, I stopped for a moment. This is probably the last time I'm ever going to wear this.'

(Trescothick on abandoning the tour of Australia in 2006.)

RATHER LIKE his batting – he stood tall, got on the front foot and attacked the bowling – Marcus Trescothick dominates the discourse about cricket and depression. In many ways, he was a trailblazer, certainly in the world of cricket, for the way he spoke publicly about his problems with mental health. He opened the batting in the dialogue of the hidden, unspoken issues of anxiety and depression of an elite sportsman or woman at a time when public admission of such a weakness would have been seen as professional suicide. As an opening batsman, Trescothick faced all the great fast bowlers of his day and never flinched, rarely letting an opportunity pass when he could make a defiant statement with his bat. He played in 76 Tests for England and averaged 43.79, an automatic choice for his country between 2000 and 2006 (when illness struck) and was named as one of *Wisden*'s Five Cricketers of the Year in 2005, the year in which he was awarded the MBE.

But it was the success of his autobiography, *Coming Back to Me,* that introduced him to a wider audience than just cricket lovers. In a searing, unsparing account of the events surrounding his abandonment of an Ashes series in Australia and his subsequent tortured descent into private despair, he laid bare the pressures and anxieties that had assailed him, he later realised, even earlier in his career, ever since he was a young boy.

The shock that this breakdown caused among his team-mates and close observers of the England team was profound. 'Tres', the cheerful boy from Somerset, the gentle giant from the West Country, everybody's friend, the bedrock upon which many an England total had been built … *ill?* Depressed? The overwhelming public response however was one of sympathy, which grew into respect with the publication of his book. Suddenly, mental health among cricketers was on everybody's lips. At last, depression was no longer a taboo subject and, with slowly gathering pace, a number of other high-profile sportsmen and women opened up about their own mental struggles. Trescothick had hit a nerve just at a time when he felt his own nerves had been shot to pieces. Deservedly his book was named the William Hill Sports Book of the Year in 2008. In the citation of the award, this was said: 'The judges felt it fearlessly tackled one of the great taboos of elite sport.'

It was inevitable therefore that he would feature front and centre in this book about cricket's depressives. Indeed, he deserved a chapter to himself, a distinction he shares with another English cricketer of great repute, the peerless Wally Hammond (though Hammond was never as popular within his own dressing room as was

Trescothick). Furthermore, Trescothick is still very much alive and continues to be involved in the game, as batting coach to the England set-up. Surely, given his public pronouncements on the subject and his encouragement of more open debate and social acknowledgement of the problem, he would be willing to speak to me. Repeated attempts to contact him met with no response, which left me puzzled and in a quandary. I couldn't discuss depression and cricket and not mention Trescothick, the most famous and high-profile of its victims. Yet he was proving elusive. Of course, he has every right to spurn my advances, and I have absolutely no problem with that. But where did it leave me?

The fact of the matter, I came to the conclusion, is that his story is already out there in the public domain. I have read his book (and very moving it is too). He has given interviews, which I have seen and read, and I have listened to the podcast he did with Luke Sutton, who has also appeared in these pages. Did I necessarily need the personal voice of Trescothick to tell his story? I wish I had but I respect his decision not to be involved. The points I wish to make, the parallels I wish to draw, the conclusions I come to, are all attainable from the material that is already to hand. So, for better or for worse, I decided to press ahead without his direct input.

Trescothick is a Somerset lad through and through. Immersed in cricket from an early age, he was playing with his father for Keynsham CC when he was 14. Tall and big for his age (he was nicknamed 'Banger' on account of his less than healthy diet that seemingly consisted of sausages with anything) meant that he could hit the ball harder and further than other lads of the same age but also brought him criticism for his 'portly' figure. The excess fat gradually fell away but the strength of shot did not. Joining Somerset in 1994, he experienced immediate success, scoring two centuries in the season and becoming a regular in the team.

Between 1995 and 2000, his county career stalled yet it was punctuated by occasional highlights. One such innings was 167 versus Glamorgan in a low-scoring match in which nobody else scored 50, which so impressed the Glamorgan coach, Duncan Fletcher, that when he was appointed England coach, he immediately called up Trescothick for the Test team. He made his debut against the West Indies in 2000. He took to Test match cricket ... well, I was about to say as readily as he took to sausages and chips but by now, he considered himself a proper professional and lived his life, including his diet, as such. Between 2001 and 2002 he was England's leading batsman and continued to make important runs at the top of the order right through until the 'Greatest Series of All Time', the Ashes victory against Australia in 2005. In his cricket career, he was riding on the crest of a wave. What could possibly go wrong?

The alarm bells – for the public, at any rate – began to ring on the Pakistan tour late in 2005, following that unforgettable Ashes win. England lost the series 2-0, disappointing in view of the heroics of the previous summer and even more so because in both matches England had been in good positions but had been unable to capitalise. Onlookers put it down to a hangover after the Ashes series and even the players later admitted they might have been a little complacent, seduced into believing that if they could beat Australia they could beat anybody.

Michael Vaughan, the side's talismanic captain, had to withdraw from the first Test, with a dodgy knee that had been plaguing him for some time and which would eventually bring to an end his international career. Trescothick was the named vice-captain on tour and now had to step into the breach. In fact, the transition was not as seamless as it seemed. Apparently, Fletcher, the coach, had reservations about Trescothick leading the side. 'Did he see something that I had not yet realised?' Trescothick later mused in his book. In the event, he took hold of the reins and, seemingly unaffected by the cares of office scored 193, which he believes was one of the best of his 13 hundreds for England, securing for his team a first-innings lead of 144. How they managed to squander that advantage to lose the Test by 22 runs is one of those imponderables that makes this game of ours so fascinating, but by then Trescothick had other things on his mind than the vagaries of a game of cricket.

On the evening of day two news came through that his father-in-law had fallen off a ladder and suffered a serious head injury. His wife, Hayley, understandably distraught at what had happened – she had discovered him unconscious in a pool of blood – begged her husband to come home. Trescothick was fearfully conflicted. He had always been a home bird – he never enjoyed being away from his family for any length of time and consequently had found touring 'difficult' – and now felt that his presence was required back in Somerset. But he was the England captain. He owed a duty of care to his team and to his country, as well as to his family.

At first, he was clear in his own mind that he should leave the tour and fly home. But it was the injured Michael Vaughan who changed his mind. He appealed to Trescothick's sense of duty, telling him that the team needed him, he had just scored 193, which had so nearly brought victory for England, and that his absence would tear a gaping hole in the batting order. Against his better judgement, Trescothick decided to stay. He justified it to himself by reasoning that, if he did abandon the tour, England would probably go into what would be the third and decisive Test without their top three batsmen in the order; Vaughan was injured, and Andrew Strauss had been given compassionate leave to return home for the birth of his first child.

On reflection, to stay was the wrong decision. 'I cannot believe I managed to persuade myself,' he wrote, 'that the England team was more important than my family.' He toughed out the rest of the tour, but he knew he was mentally exhausted. On his return to Birmingham Airport, his family came to greet him, and his eight-month-old daughter didn't recognise him. 'I'd been away for two and a half months. I remember holding her in my arms and she was looking at me as if to say, who the hell are you? And I hated it. It was a horrible feeling.'

The treadmill of an international cricketer is relentless. In February 2006, England were once more boarding a plane, this time to India. Trescothick had been feeling the familiar pangs of homesickness even before the plane took off, but he assumed things would settle down – as they usually did throughout the previous ten years of touring – but duty called, and England needed him. Even more so when Vaughan's knee flared up again and he was declared unfit to play in the first Test. Once more, Trescothick, as vice-captain, took charge of the team, yet he knew he wasn't up to it. His mind was simply incapable of coping. He barely remembers the first day's play. He spent a restless night, with all sorts of terrible imaginings and deeply upsetting thoughts assailing him. Much more than pre-match nerves, this was something he had never experienced. 'I started sweating heavily,' he wrote. 'I started shaking. I felt myself losing control. I was petrified.'

How he got through the second day's play – and he was captain – he never knew. Another troubled and sleepless night followed. Strauss later admitted to him that, on the bus to the ground for day three, he had never seen anybody looking so ill. Mechanically, Trescothick strapped on his pads and somehow reached 35 without remembering a single shot he played. 'I never saw the ball that got me out,' he wrote. Back in the dressing room, he broke down and wept uncontrollably. Through his sobs, he told the management he couldn't go on any longer; he had to go home.

That much had been clear to everybody who was there. Arrangements were made, a flight organised and, as swiftly and unobtrusively as possible, he was on his way home. He slept deeply on the nine-hour flight and driving back to Taunton from Heathrow, he filled up his diesel car with petrol. He realised, as he succinctly put it, he was in 'a sort of hell'.

'I just didn't have a clue what was happening to me, or why. All I knew is that I couldn't deal with it, because I didn't really know what it was I was supposed to be dealing with, let alone how. I felt like something, or someone, was taking over my mind and my body and was trying to destroy me.'

He needed help – he was sure about that – so he asked his GP if he could be admitted to hospital and for the first time in any of his dealings with doctors, he heard the word 'depression' used. In common with just about everybody who has suffered with the complaint, at first the diagnosis is hard to take in. *Depression?* What on earth was there to be depressed about? He was an opening batsman, for heaven's sake – depression is for weak people, and weak people don't go toe to toe with the world's fastest bowlers. Nonetheless, he took the drugs that were prescribed for him. Perhaps the edge of the pain was smoothed off, but life became a blur; 'I was drugged up to the eyeballs,' he remembers, 'wandering around the house like a zombie.' Strong medication for depression can act like this; there is always a balancing act to perform. Not enough drugs and everyday life becomes unbearable; too much and you cease to function as a person.

Having fallen off the horse so publicly and spectacularly, the plan – his plan – was to climb back into the saddle as soon as possible. Once the English domestic season began, he started to feel better. Or, at least, he was convincing himself he was getting better. Vaughan rang to enquire how he was and whether there was any possibility of his making the summer Tests, against Sri Lanka and Pakistan. He lied. Not the most sensible course of action but even now, after all he had been through, he was unwilling to admit publicly, even to his friend and captain, Michael Vaughan, that his illness persisted.

He may have been unwilling to come clean about what was really wrong with him but the press were insatiable in their quest to discover the real reason for his abandoning the tour of India. The ECB organised a press conference, in which Trescothick would be led gently through a series of planned questions. Ian Ward, a former player himself and now a commentator for Sky, led the interview. In it, Trescothick blamed a virus for his being forced home from India, assured Ward that he was planning to play in all the Tests that summer and far from giving up his England career, his stated intent was to play 100 Test matches. None of it was true, of course. Michael Atherton, a former England opener with Trescothick, now writing in *The Sunday Telegraph*, immediately smelt a rat. The line about the virus 'was so utterly implausible that ridicule is the only response'. The whole charade was nothing less than a cover-up. Atherton was not the only onlooker who wasn't fooled.

Why? Why did Trescothick not tell the truth? That is a question he struggles to answer, even now, looking back, let alone at the time. Here, he touches upon the dilemma that all of us who have suffered from this illness have to face up to at some time; do we openly admit to our problem, or do we dissemble and pretend that it is something else that afflicts us? A 'virus', in Trescothick's case, or a 'stress-related illness', in Trott's, or 'personal problems' in countless other cases, or whatever excuse we make up in order not to go public with the true cause. For no matter how much we are encouraged not to dissemble, whatever good and convincing arguments that are placed before us not to pretend, it takes a strong man or woman to come clean, especially in front of the whole world, when the merciless beam of 'public interest' is shone in our face. There is still that stigma attached to mental illness in spite of herculean efforts on the part of sufferers and their consultants and counsellors to break the mould; there is still a feeling that judgement is being handed down. Rather like the suspicion of cheating in an examination or in a quiz show or in golf by moving your marker inches towards the hole or not 'walking' at cricket, it hangs about you like a bad smell. Probably best not to admit to it; you might be dropped for the next game because it was felt that you were mentally frail, you were a bit 'flaky', not up to the task.

So Trescothick pretended he was fine, when clearly in his own mind he was not. There was a summer's cricket to get through and he had to strap on his pads and make some runs if he was going to be selected for that winter's tour of Australia. An Ashes tour down under is the apogee of any Englishman's career and he could not possibly miss that. Yet he was fully aware that the Sky interview had been an unmitigated disaster, fooling nobody, so he rang Richard Bevan, the chief executive of the Professional Cricketers' Association, asking for help. Immediately, he was put in touch with a Cognitive Behaviour Therapist (a talking counsellor) who led him through a number of sessions, which explored every facet of his life, looking for what are called 'triggers', possible reasons for his depression.

As is their way, the therapist took him right back to his childhood and it became increasingly apparent to Trescothick that he had always suffered from acute homesickness even from a young age. Away matches that necessitated a night, or more than one night, away from home, had become a torment. He had coped – or thought he had coped – by castigating himself for being such a baby. As time wore on, he came to realise that these moods of loneliness and isolation would pass once matches got underway and he could immerse himself in the fun and camaraderie of life in a dressing room or on tour, but these feelings never really went away. Touring became harder and he found that he was beginning to despise himself. What on earth have I got to worry about, he tried to tell himself. I'm playing for England; others would bite my hand off for the same privilege.

Once Trescothick started to pour out his emotions of self-abnegation, his feelings of worthlessness and anger at not being able to get a grip, his therapist held up a hand to stop him. He was told in no uncertain terms – I remember the same words being spoken to me – that depression was *not his fault*. A broken leg is put in plaster; everybody can see what the problem is. A patient can have heart surgery; he can show the scar to prove it. A bowler can pull up lame; as he limps off the field, everybody knows what has happened. But depression is a hidden illness, and most sufferers are not anxious to share their problems with the world at large. More often than not, they soldier on, putting a brave face on things, before – inevitably – they hit the buffers. One psychiatrist said to me, 'The phrase "*man up*" should be banned!'

Trescothick, now less inclined to beat himself up for his inability to do just that, had to admit that he was exhausted, mentally, physically and emotionally. For six years, he had been on the international treadmill, constantly playing, training and travelling with England, always under the microscope of public scrutiny whilst performing at the highest level. No wonder your body – and your mind – is in revolt he was told, and crying out for some respite.

It was not just international cricketers at risk, nor more broadly elite sportsmen and women in any category; anybody in a position of huge responsibility and intense scrutiny is subject to the same pressures. Trescothick was introduced to a book written by the psychiatrist, Dr Tim Cantopher, *Depressive Illness: The Curse of the Strong*. Its message lay in its title. The myth that people who get depressed are in some way weak is one he is anxious to explode. In fact, the opposite is true. A depressive is usually strong, reliable and diligent with a highly developed sense of responsibility but paradoxically easily hurt and affected by criticism. He or she may have a self-esteem that appears robust on the surface, but underneath is vulnerable.

That's me, Trescothick admitted to himself, secretly quite relieved on two counts. One, he was reassured that no, he was not going mad; there was a cause for his feelings of desperation, and it had a clinical diagnosis. And secondly, he was consoled by the list of famous people who had suffered from the illness: Oliver Cromwell, Abraham Lincoln, Isaac Newton, Vincent van Gogh, Ernest Hemingway, Winston Churchill and many, many others.

'The road to recovery,' he wrote, 'would be long and anything but straight,' but for the first time he was able to hold on to that word 'recovery'. Feeling more at ease with himself, he was anxious to get back to doing what he had been born to do, start playing county cricket again. But not sufficiently at ease with himself to come clean with the nation's press as to what it was exactly that had forced him home early from the tour of India. The newshounds had smelt a rat and once they believed there was a story lurking behind the bland pronouncements from the ECB, they were relentless in their pursuit of the truth. In retrospect, Trescothick should not have sought to evade the issue, but it is perfectly understandable why he did not want it plastered all over the back pages. In the meantime, he said that 'burn-out' was the cause and hoped that the problem would simply go away. Of course, it did not. It smouldered and then burst into flames at the worst time possible.

He scored a hundred for Somerset and convinced himself he felt a lot better. Duncan Fletcher rang to enquire about his fitness for the forthcoming home Test matches. 'Are you okay to play?' he asked. 'Yes,' Trescothick replied. The die was cast. There was no going back now.

He was duly selected for all the Test matches that summer against Sri Lanka and Pakistan and scored a memorable hundred at Lord's. His gamble, if that was what you called it, seemed to be paying off. Not only was he surviving in the hot-house environment of Test match cricket, but he was thriving; rarely can he have batted better. He wrote: 'Walking back to a standing ovation was a sublime moment. Not long before, when my depressive illness was at its most powerful, my future had appeared so bleak to me to be almost impossible to bear.'

It was too good to last. Before the next Test, an article appeared in *The News of the World*, uncovering the cover-up, as it were, accusing the cricket authorities of leading the press and the public up the garden path with palpably untrue communiques. Trescothick, they had been assured, had returned from India owing to 'personal reasons', intimating that domestic issues were to blame, when clearly, they were not. One can only imagine Trescothick's dismay, having his state of mind so publicly scrutinised and pored over, when all he wanted was to be left alone so that he could concentrate on what he was there to do, to score runs for England.

Strangely, once the cat was out of the bag, press interest seemed to die down and the furore blew over. Nobody really had it in for Trescothick. He was a loyal servant of his country's cricket team, he was an integral part of the batting unit, he had helped to win back the Ashes after all those years of hurt and, if he had mental issues, something that was only recently beginning to gnaw away at the public consciousness, public opinion was broadly on his side. If depression had not yet been wholly accepted as a 'genuine' illness, neither was it something which even the more sensational of the third estate were comfortable denouncing. Trescothick, 'Tresco' to his team-mates, was not a conspicuous target. He was left untroubled – except, of course, by his own misgivings and inner demons.

Besides, the press had lighted upon another story. It had become increasingly obvious, following several attempts at a comeback, that Michael Vaughan was not going to lead England to Australia on the forthcoming Ashes series that winter. His troublesome knee had let him down one time too many. Who was going to captain the side? Trescothick favoured Andrew Strauss but in the end, perhaps against his better judgement, Trescothick hints, Fletcher opted for Andrew Flintoff … and we all know how well that turned out. In a sense, Trescothick was relieved that press attention had been diverted from him because he had to prepare himself, both physically and mentally, for the searching examination ahead. It wasn't going to be easy – no tour of Australia is, no matter how resilient your temperament – but he believed, in view of how well he had performed in the summer Tests, that he was equal to the task. 'I was definitely feeling better and more able to understand the process of my illness, how it worked and what it was, and I was much more comfortable with the idea that people would handle the truth without thinking too badly of me.'

His confidence, as we know now, was misplaced.

As the plane carrying the England team touched down on Australian soil and as they went through the preliminary media scrum and press conference and sought the sanctuary of their hotel, they were all taken aback by their reception. Trescothick had been on a previous Ashes tour in 2002/03 and was fully prepared for hot encounters on the field of play but had always reckoned that the Aussies were a fairly decent bunch over a beer or two at the close of play. But this was different. Following their loss to England in the Greatest Ashes Series Ever in 2005, they were desperate to regain the urn. Nothing wrong with that, but Trescothick was surprised at the level of belligerence and hostility aimed at the England team … and this was before a ball had been bowled. 'They didn't just want revenge,' he wrote, 'they wanted annihilation.'

History records that annihilation of the England team is exactly what they got. Flintoff was unable to repeat his heroics of 2005, the tour swiftly unravelled, and Australia secured the whitewash (5-0) that they craved. All this drama and heartache passed Trescothick by. His illness returned with a vengeance and for the second time – and the last – he was forced to abandon ship and return home. The details of his mental collapse make for difficult reading.

The first game of the tour, no more than a pipe-opener, against the Prime Minister's XI at Canberra, was not the start to an Ashes campaign that the England team would have wished for; they were thrashed. Nobody remembers these initial skirmishes, but they tend to set the tone for what is to come. For Trescothick, a rising tide of panic threatened to overwhelm him. All the old, familiar signs of anxiety, dread, homesickness and sleeplessness were back, and he knew he was heading for a breakdown.

The remaining 72 hours of his tour remain a blur. The first serious outing of the tour was against New South Wales. England lost the toss and all Trescothick can remember of that day in the field was dropping a sitter at slip. Next day, he played his last innings for England. It was 'a scrappy non-event', as he described it in his book, 'which ended when I dragged one on from Brett Lee.' That night, he didn't sleep a wink. He tried all the calming and rationalising techniques he had been taught but nothing worked. 'And now I had let everyone down. I said I was all right and I wasn't … and on and on and here I go again. Oh God! Make it stop!'

How he made it through breakfast the next morning, the coach journey to the ground and some warm-ups before fielding, he doesn't know. 'All day long in the field, the feelings had been growing more and more intense. And then, as if someone flicked a switch, I knew it was over. I asked the umpire if I could go off for a leak … and never came back.'

Having reached the sanctuary of the dressing room, he broke down and sobbed uncontrollably. When the team came in for tea, he was ushered into the physio's room, whilst frantic planning by the management for his immediate repatriation took place. After the team had gone out after tea, Trescothick gathered up his kit and packed his bag.

'Perhaps the saddest moment of all came when I picked up my England cap to put it in my bag. The thought of what I was doing and of what it might mean hit me like a kick in the guts … As I placed the navy-blue cap with the three lions in my bag, I stopped for a moment. This is probably the last moment I'm ever going to wear this. I just felt empty. The moment seemed so final.' It was indeed final. In March 2008, at the age of 32, with 76 Test caps, he announced his retirement from international cricket.

Trescothick may have been unwilling to talk to me, but he did talk to Luke Sutton, who appears elsewhere in these pages and who encouraged me to listen to one of his podcasts in which he encourages Trescothick to speak about his mental health issues. It helped of course that Trescothick and Sutton were old friends; they were both born in Keynsham in Somerset, they were almost exact contemporaries, and both had shadowed each other up the age groups and into the Somerset team. No doubt the closeness of their relationship encouraged Trescothick to have the confidence to open up and to be honest in his self-analysis; he spoke well, occasionally quite movingly, with nothing, it would appear, off limits.

The first point Sutton made was that it had come as a complete surprise when he heard of his friend's depression; he had no idea that Trescothick had been struggling from an early age. That struck a chord with me; depressives are notoriously good actors and in the main like to pretend that the sun is shining, and all is well with the world – our world. Then Trescothick described how he felt on that ill-fated tour of India, his feeling ill, his sense of isolation hiding in his hotel room, his panic because he knew something was drastically wrong, but he did not know what. He could confide in no one because the public perception of mental illness was still in the Dark Ages. Besides, an open admission of emotional, as opposed to physical, breakdown was tantamount to a declaration of weakness, and no international cricketer could afford to cede the upper hand to his opponents. What would the coach say? Would the captain be prepared to go into battle with one who was perceived to be flaky? No, Trescothick preferred to sort it out himself … with disastrous consequences, as he painfully found out.

Nowadays, we have a much better understanding of the problem, he insisted, and have progressed enormously in our treatment of those afflicted. Before, if somebody started having the same tribulations as he had, the scornful response of the less sympathetic would have been 'he's losing the plot'. What plot? There is no plot. Nobody consciously plots a course through life to include – or even to avoid – mental turmoil. Stuff happens.

Sutton introduced the theory that depression is the 'curse of the strong'. Are high-performance athletes more prone? Those who are incredibly strong mentally, those who attain the pinnacle of their profession, often reach a tipping point, while others without the same drive and ambition do not get to the top and do not tip over. His friend, Trescothick, was dedicated to the England team and did not want to let down his team-mates. Jonathan Trott, who suffered similar problems, was a tough competitor and drove himself to extract every last ounce out of his talents until he had nothing left to give. Both men, Sutton concluded, had been pressing the revs too many times and the engine had simply blown.

But it had always been with me, Trescothick insisted, and called to mind an under-14 Somerset tour of Holland, for which both he and Sutton had been selected, and even as far back as then, he had struggled with homesickness. In fact, he recalled being anxious about being away from home as young as ten. So, all these feelings of anxiety, panic and sleeplessness, right up until well into his England days, he ascribed to homesickness. He was missing his wife and children. It was not until that Indian tour that he began to suspect that it was something worse.

Once again, Sutton postulated … is somebody who suffers from depression predisposed to the condition, is it in the genes, or is it life's experiences that is the culprit? A bit of both, Trescothick answered, and then added to the mix the spectre of Covid and its effects of social isolation and loneliness. He marvelled at the way teams have been able to cope with 'bubbles' and competing in empty stadiums. At the time the virus struck, Trescothick was employed as England's batting coach. He recalled the two Test matches at the Rose Bowl and Old Trafford (chosen because both grounds had a hotel on site) and felt keenly – they all did – the impossibility of enjoying relaxing pleasures such a coffee, a meal, a round of golf during their downtime. 'And we were in our own country!' he cried. 'The Pakistanis were a long way from home.'

Going back to his own troubles. Trescothick said he was desperate to get back to playing for England after the Indian debacle. He had played a summer of Tests before going to Australia and felt he had coped well enough. But the minute he stepped off the plane in Australia with the England team all the old feelings of panic and despair came flooding back. In retrospect, he said, he should not have gone and given himself the winter off to recover properly. The subsequent decision to retire from international cricket he believed to have been the right one.

How are you now? Sutton asked. Fine, was the reply. If ever he feels on edge, he takes his medication – it helps to calm him down. For him, the best way of coping is a combination of medication and talking therapy. At least he knows what is wrong and how to deal with it.

Do you score your mood? asked Sutton. No, answered Trescothick, because he did not want to burden his wife with a daily ready reckoner. He has been told to talk about his feelings, he encourages others to do so but admits he's still not very good at doing it himself. But his wife reads him like a book; she can gauge his mood. Especially if he's off his food, he added. That evinced a laugh from his friend.

Following the publication of his book and the almost universal praise it generated, Trescothick said that from time to time ex-players, even current ones, approach him for a chat and some sympathetic encouragement. Coaches today are much more aware of the problem and are taught to look out for the tell-tale signs in their charges. The ones to worry about, he said, are the ones like him, those who do not confide in their team-mates, those who refuse to believe that anything is wrong with them … until it is too late.

It's good – it's best – to talk, both agreed, as the podcast was brought to a close. The interview between old friends had brought me as close as I had hoped in understanding how Trescothick had tried to manage his situation. Probably better than my interviewing him myself.

Chapter 9

Helping Hands

The Professional Cricketers' Association (PCA)

IT WAS as late on in the game's history as 1968 that professional cricketers in England set up their first trade union. From the first stirrings of cricket in this country as a professional sport in the 18th century, to becoming the nation's number one game in the mid to late 19th century, it began to enjoy levels of interest and popularity that have rarely been surpassed. Bestriding the game like a Colossus was none other than the gargantuan figure of the Bearded One himself. It was often claimed, not without justification, that W.G. Grace was the most easily recognisable figure in the land, including Queen Victoria, who had to all intents and purposes retired from public life after the death of her husband, Prince Albert, in 1861 and was rarely seen by her public. Not for nothing were the years prior to the First World War known as the Golden Age of Cricket. Players such as Andrew Stoddart, Archie MacLaren, Stanley Jackson, C.B. Fry, R.E. Foster, Prince Ranjitsinhji, R.H. Spooner, Gilbert Jessop, Jack Hobbs, Frank Woolley *et al* were the rock gods of their age, or Hollywood stars of a later age, and the British public flocked in their thousands to watch them play. Needless to say, all these great players were batsmen and perforce amateurs; the donkey work, the bowling, was largely performed by the professionals, men like George Hirst, Wilfred Rhodes, Sydney Barnes, Tom Richardson, George Lohmann, J.T. Hearne, Johnny Briggs and Bobby Peel, wonderful practitioners all of their craft, but woefully underpaid. W.G. incidentally played under the *aegis* of an amateur, but everybody knew and understood that the wily old man earned much more from playing the game than probably the rest of the professionals put together. He was the original 'shamateur', a splendid example of the typical British predilection for compromise and hypocrisy.

You would have expected that following the First World War, class divisions within British society would have largely crumbled. After all, how could men who had fought alongside their officers in the trenches be expected to change in separate rooms and exit on to the field of play through different gates once county cricket resumed after the cessation of hostilities? But that was how it was and that is how it remained. Those with private means played as amateurs and the rest, the professionals, had to shift for themselves. Even the 'Master', Jack Hobbs, generally regarded as England's finest batsman, was dependent on continued employment at the whims of the Surrey cricket committee and needed to augment his relatively meagre wages by lending his name to various commercial products. To the end of his lengthy and glittering career, his thoughts were forever on securing a future for his family. Job security, a fair wage, personal insurance, a voice on the committee, redress for unfair treatment or dismissal? There was none. Even the Second World War brought about little change or reform in the corridors of power at Lord's. The MCC had its tight grip on the levers of power in the early 1950s as much as the Lords Hawke and Harris had wielded their unelected power decades earlier.

Yet change, tortoise-like no doubt, was coming. The central figure in this perennial endeavour for greater status for professionals was Hobbs's successor as England's greatest batsman, Len Hutton (though fans of Wally Hammond could easily lay a counter-claim to that accolade). In the immediate post-war years, Hutton stood head and shoulders above any of his contemporaries as a batsman. Until he finally hung up his boots in 1955, England relied heavily upon him for runs, a burden of responsibility which he found overwhelming at times, especially in the face of relentless fast bowling from the fearsome Australian pace duo of Ray Lindwall and Keith Miller.

Two tours to Australia after the war, in 1946/47 and 1950/51, lost disastrously 3-0 and 4-1 respectively, brought it home to the British public and – reluctantly – to the Test selectors that only one man was capable of leading England out of the doldrums and that was Len Hutton. The trouble was that Hutton was a professional, and professionals historically did not captain England. Yet none of the existing serving amateur captains of the counties was remotely suitable to lead the Test team and accordingly – and possibly a tad warily – the selectors broke with long-established custom and appointed Hutton. He repaid their faith by regaining the Ashes in England in 1953 after 20 years of disappointment. Furthermore, he led England to success in the following Ashes encounter down under in 1954/55.

That was it. He had shot his bolt. Emotionally and physically drained, he retired from the game and the reins of office were handed over to Peter May, Charterhouse, Cambridge and Surrey, an amateur. English cricket was returning to type. Well, not quite. Though an amateur, and popularly regarded as England's finest post-war batsman (that is until the emergence of Joe Root), May had watched and learned under Hutton and brought to his captaincy a hard-edged and ruthless philosophy that was just as 'professional' as the professional Hutton. The distinctions between amateur and professional of the game in England were starting to blur and by 1962 were done away with altogether, reflecting a seismic change in society. A more egalitarian culture was prevailing after the privations of war; the Swinging Sixties was not led by toffs and establishment figures, but by young people with money to spend and no heed to tradition. Modernity and fun-loving hedonism transformed the country, and especially its capital, from a gloomy, grimy, post-war world into a bright, new, shiny epicentre of style and libertarianism. Was cricket swift to embrace the brave new world of the Beatles, the Rolling Stones, the Who, the Kinks, Mary Quant and the miniskirt and the colourful fashion of Carnaby Street and the Kings Road? Or, to put it another way, was cricket throwing off its centuries-old shackles of exploitation of the workers – the hard-up professional players on minimum wages – by the ruling classes at Lord's and in committee rooms at county grounds the length and breadth of the land?

Not willingly and not quickly was the simple answer. Cricketers needed to get their act together, form themselves in to a collective, a union, the better to negotiate higher wages and better working conditions, as manual workers had done over a century before. The time was now ripe for the birth of the Professional Cricketers' Association.

Rather like his bowling, left-arm over the wicket and distinctly fast, it was Fred Rumsey, at that time taking stacks of wickets for Somerset, who was leading the charge for unionisation. He had first started his career at Worcestershire before moving to Somerset, where his rumbustious bowling had caught the eyes of the national selectors who picked him for a total of five Tests in the mid-1960s. Over beers in the pavilion bar after the close of play, he had discussed with team-mates and opponents the shocking fact that the players, those who pulled the spectators through the turnstiles and put a show on for the paying customers, had absolutely no say in the running of the game. It was positively Victorian, they agreed, and looking back from today's perspective that was no exaggeration. Unusually for a fast bowler, Rumsey was disinclined to put his feet up after a day's play, even if it had involved bowling plenty of overs – he had a much too restless mind for that. He was already the public relations and fundraising officer at Somerset and now he applied his organisational and personal skills to full advantage and canvassed support from his many contacts in the game for the formation of a cricketers' union. He met with nothing other than overwhelming enthusiasm for the project.

From the players, that is. The powers-that-be at Lord's, together with their acolytes on the county committees, rapidly erected what obstacles they could, which were plenty and formidable. Yet they were, Canute like, attempting to stem a tide that was inexorably on the turn. Cricket was changing. In a bid to arrest falling gates and loss of popular interest in the County Championship, new one-day competitions were being mooted. The Gillette Cup had proved to be a roaring success and plans were in the pipeline for a Sunday League and the new Benson and Hedges Cup. If the players had no say in the restructuring of the domestic game, Rumsey argued, the governance of professional cricket would be taking a step backwards into the Dark Ages. Wages were being paid that had fallen below the national average. Contracts only covered six months of the year with no provision for employment throughout the winter months. There was no personal insurance cover in a trade where injury was an occupational hazard. And all this in an era when it seemed to some observers that it was not the government that was running the country but the Trades Union Congress. Cricket seemed wildly out of step with the times.

Accordingly, Rumsey wrote to all 17 (as they were then) first-class counties, outlining his plans for an association, one that the game sorely needed. Employing his contacts as a public relations officer, he enlisted the support of *The Daily Express* to sponsor their first meeting at the Press Club in London. The meeting was chaired by the Sussex and England wicketkeeper, Jim Parks, a personable fellow, who possessed the happy knack of getting everybody on board, though he made it plain he would only fulfil the role temporarily until such time as a more permanent figure should be appointed. The chair was subsequently taken by Jack Bannister, a seat he kept warm for the next 20 years. The meeting was addressed by Jimmy Hill, who had blazed a trail for footballers' rights when he became the first chairman of the Professional Footballers' Association in 1957 and led the opposition to the feudal maximum wage of £20 a week, which was finally scrapped in 1961, allowing Fulham's Johnny Haynes to become the first £100-a-week footballer.

Where football had started, cricket followed. A proper professional association had to be formed but who should be its first president? The choice of John Arlott, the passionate advocate of the ordinary first-class cricketer, could not have been more inspired. He was humbled to be so honoured and worked tirelessly in those early years as the Professional Cricketers' Association found its feet and its voice.

It was at this time that I was tentatively dipping my toes into the professional game, albeit only as an undergraduate on a summer contract with Hampshire for £10 a week (I didn't know what Johnny Haynes had to worry about). To be truthful, all I was interested in was playing cricket … and, *mirabile dictu*, getting paid for it, while my university friends were scrambling around for holiday jobs to augment their termly grant. I had no idea the PCA existed. We were not encouraged to join. Nobody came to talk to us. We received no official correspondence and nobody in the dressing room climbed up on a soapbox to lead us to the light. Hampshire did not even provide soap for the showers so nowhere was there to be found a soapbox. Clearly, the PCA had missionary work to be done.

It was Packer who changed all that, as he changed so much about the game. When the bombshell exploded in our faces in 1977, and it became clear that his pirate World Series Cricket was going to hijack all the world's best players, most of whom were already playing in England's County Championship, the uncomfortable question had to be addressed: should they be allowed to play in our domestic competitions, or should they be banned? The matter was hotly debated in dressing rooms up and down the country. Tempers flared, friendships and loyalties were tested and rifts opened up. We at Hampshire had three WSC players in our ranks – Barry Richards, Andy Roberts and Gordon Greenidge – and you can safely say that the atmosphere at the club became, if not sulphurous, then a little strained. As for the rest of us, those who had not been approached by Packer, including our team joker who kept on pretending that he had to take an important telephone call from Australia, were encouraged – 'sent' might be a better word – to Edgbaston to attend an Extraordinary General Meeting of the PCA to discuss this very matter and how it would impact on the professional game in this country. The meeting was packed. Everybody was there.

The ins and outs of the Packer Revolution and the role the PCA played in trying to act as a mediator between the banned players and the Test and County Cricket Board do not concern us here. What was inescapable, however, looking around at the massed ranks of the great and the good of English cricket, was that the PCA, now having got its act together, was a powerful and influential beast indeed. It had arrived. Not long afterwards, I had retired and the workings of the organisation, spreading its benign but powerful influence into every nook and cranny of the game of cricket, both professional and recreational, largely passed me by. Occasional upheavals, scandals, crises in the game would bring the organisation to the forefront of public awareness, but for the most part, its work, always for good, always altruistic, often philanthropic, went under the radar.

That is until I started writing this book. Depression and cricket had become a hot topic with the publication of Marcus Trescothick's book and I wondered what the organisation, set up specifically to safeguard the welfare of cricketers, was offering by way of support to sufferers of this illness and for those charged with looking after them, their employers, the clubs.

The short answer is quite a lot.

Their website is glossy, exhaustive, and very much in vogue. It attempts to cover just about every scenario in the personal development and welfare of cricketers, and all the cliches, straplines and buzzwords with which I have become familiar in my own dealings with the world of depression, are there in abundance. I do not mean this as a derogatory observation, simply that what was once a bit of a hidden affliction has now become very much mainstream. Nonetheless, like all large organisations, it does like to wrap itself in overblown and grandiloquent language. Take this item under the heading 'Corporate – Lumina Spark in groups and 1-1 to build self-awareness, confidence, team cohesion and improve absenteeism.' I can just imagine the reception that would have got in the Hampshire dressing room of the 1970s, not a place well-known for introspection and navel-gazing. Lumina Spark? Who does he play for? But that was probably the problem with that generation, an inclination to scoff in order not to show weakness (though I was unaware that absenteeism has ever been a problem in the game; if you didn't pitch up in time you were dropped and your future as a cricketer short-lived).

Nevertheless, putting building blocks in place to help cricketers with mental health issues is a laudable project and, from anecdotal evidence, it would seem that the PCA has been very active in several well-known, and many more not so well-known, cases where help has been sought and help has been given. Depression of course is not the sole problem afflicting professional cricketers. Stress, alcohol, drugs, gambling, self-harm … all the self-destructive habits that the human flesh is heir to, are identified, explained and analysed, with aid and advice provided.

But it is depression that is the subject of this book and the PCA cannot be accused of not taking the subject seriously. Tutorials, seminars, programmes, helplines, self-help tools, clinics, presentations, counselling, consultations and links to sister organisations abound. It makes me think how on earth professional cricketers of earlier eras ever managed to step on to the field of play, seeing as these buttresses were not yet in existence, but of course some found themselves unable to do so and many more suffered in silence. My admiration knows no bounds for those of a more recent vintage who have stood up and admitted their pain and their burden in public. Several high-profile names have accepted ambassadorial roles in raising awareness of depression; among their number are Andrew Flintoff, Marcus Trescothick, Graeme Fowler, Monty Panesar, Tim Ambrose and Mike Yardy. A sadness for me is that only Graeme Fowler answered my request to tell his own story in these pages. That is a pity, an opportunity to promote their good work missed.

I was encouraged to talk to Ian Thomas, one of the directors at the PCA, and he was most willing to expound about his work and the support that the Association provide in mental health in the professional game. Our conversation ranged widely across many of the well-known cases that have entered the public domain … and many that haven't. Clearly, individual confidentiality precluded him from giving me names to contact with a view to their telling their story. 'But what about the recreational game?' he said. 'This is a problem that affects club cricketers too.' That I had not considered and rapidly came to the conclusion that I had better cast my net wider.

To expound on his theme, he recounted his own experience of the pernicious effect cricket can have on some poor, lost souls in the recreational game. Alun Thomas played for Newport CC, a ground I remember, having played there against Glamorgan many years ago. He was a talented club cricketer, a good mate of his namesake, the aforesaid

Ian Thomas, and took his own life in 2018. According to Ian, Alun was Mr Newport: player, groundsman, president, teller of tall tales and humorous anecdotes. Apparently, he had been in a bad way in the months leading up to his death, but he had avoided seeking help believing (probably correctly) that the NHS was ill-equipped to provide the necessary support and guidance. 'The older generation were brought up not to make a fuss,' Ian pointed out, seemingly oblivious to the fact that I was firmly in this age bracket myself, but I nodded in agreement. He was only telling the truth. Alun Thomas lived for his cricket and when the season finished and the long winter evenings started to draw in, he would sink into the slough of despond. 'The irony of Alun's suicide,' Ian said, 'was that I was working on this self-same topic with the PCA, as I felt that we had been negligent in bringing mental health front and centre of our work.' His line of thought was that cricket is a seasonal sport and for those who live and breathe for the game, the winter months can be a dangerous time.

In order to further my research, I contacted Huw Turbervill, the editor of *The Cricketer*. I have had contact with him in the past but there is another reason that prompted my call. He plays for Beddington Cricket Club in Surrey and Beddington happened to be my local club when I was at school. I have nothing but happy memories of weekends playing on their delightful ground, often accompanied by the pleasing ringing of the neighbouring church bells. Beddington was where I learnt to play the game. It was also where I grew up, playing alongside men, good cricketers all, who taught me as much about life as how to play a cover drive. Huw was only too pleased to add his pennyworth to the relationship between cricket and depression.

The camaraderie provided by playing in a team, he said, is the same for a club cricketer as it is for a professional. In some ways, he contended, the sense of belonging can be even more intense. Weekend cricket can be a welcome relief from a humdrum existence during the week. It can be an escape from a boring job, from a suffocating domestic situation, from mundane daily chores, from a lonely personal life. For many, the weekend's cricket is an oasis, eagerly anticipated in the days leading up to a match. For some, it can become all-consuming. Consider those club stalwarts, who generously give of their time, working on the ground, mowing the outfield, serving behind the bar, volunteering for administrative duties, organising nets, painting the changing rooms. Cricket clubs rely on such servants but, by the same token, members rely on the club to give them a distraction, a passion, a *raison d'etre.* And then, all of a sudden, far too soon, it shuts up shop for the winter and there is nothing for it but to pine for the next season. It is depressing enough for the emotionally robust club cricketer. For the character prone to melancholy, it can be a thoroughly bleak prospect.

Furthermore, Huw pointed out, the club cricketer is subject to the same vagaries of form, selection, injury, the passing of the years, just as any professional. Because an enforced period of time out of the game, short or extended, is not a potential loss of livelihood, as it would be with a professional cricketer, does not mean that the privation is any the less keenly felt. Club cricketers too feel anxious about their place in the team and worry about their performances. You can get out for a duck on a Saturday and not pick up a bat until the following Saturday. Sometimes you can pick up your bat on the following Saturday but not wield it in anger because your captain has declared just as you are about to strap on your pads. And then it might rain the next Saturday and you have gone a month without an innings. Whatever form you might, or might not, have been in has vanished into thin air. Huw admitted that he begins to feel anxious about the forthcoming Saturday fixture on Thursday. The stresses and strains, the fear of failure, the frustrations at what is a difficult and complex game, are as intense for the club cricketer as for the county player. Thus, I was disabused of my naïve belief that club cricketers only play for 'fun'. They may not be professionals, they do not play every day, their livelihood does not depend on their performances, but they take the game (well, most of them) every bit as seriously as any county player.

Then Ian Thomas encouraged me to get in touch with somebody he knows in the recreational game, who has taken an interest in the subject of mental health among club cricketers. Mark Boyns has set up his own support organisation, Opening Up Cricket, to tour cricket clubs with a view to airing the subject – hitherto not a terribly hot topic in club pavilions – among the amateurs of our game. The genesis of his campaign, he told me when I contacted him, was the suicide of his great friend and team-mate at Sefton Park CC in Liverpool. After a period of mourning and reflection ('could I have foreseen what was going to happen and what could I have done to prevent it?' – the natural response of family and friends in the aftermath of such a shock), Boyns began to understand that this tragedy was not a one-off. The more he discussed it with friends and colleagues, the more he came to appreciate that suicide is not uncommon among young men. Ergo, it seemed self-evident that he ought to use his experience, notwithstanding its painful memories, to open up (the pun in the organisation's name is clearly deliberate) the discussion about depression and mental health to a much wider audience. What better vehicle for this project, he reasoned, could there possibly be than through cricket clubs? Alex Miller, the lad who took his own life, was 'nuts about cricket', as Boyns put it. 'Whatever problems Alex had,' he said, 'and obviously he had many, though they were not apparent to us, his team-mates, he could put to one side during the summer months. Cricket gave him a focus which he didn't have during the winter.' *So, cricket was a panacea, not the cause, of his distress?* Boyns gave this some thought. 'Yes, probably. But you could say the *absence* of cricket during those long dark winter months could have contributed to his distress.'

Boyns concluded that proactive, rather than reactive, action was needed here. Accordingly, with help from like-minded friends, he took to visiting cricket clubs in the area to talk about Alex and to encourage those who were struggling themselves to seek help and support. Resources were available, he told them, and slowly, by word of mouth more than anything else, he and his band of brothers were finding themselves much in demand. 'We now have a dozen people working for Opening Up Cricket. I'm fortunate in that my day job is as a teacher. I teach four days a week, there are the long holidays, and I have time to go round clubs to spread the word.' *What exactly is the 'word'?* 'We deliver sessions of varying length and content. They include seminars on developing mental skills for cricket, wellbeing, looking out for team-mates, coping with disappointment and setbacks, dealing with stress and pressure. Our aim is to speak to local cricketers about my experience of losing a much-loved team-mate to suicide and how such tragedies might be averted.'

The reception, the feedback, following such meetings has been very good, he said. *Have you had any resistance from those who believe that all this talk about mental health is so much nonsense? You know, the sort of people who advocate a stiff upper lip in the face of misfortune, who say 'man up' or 'get over it?'* 'Not much. I guess that as these meetings are advertised by the clubs, anyone who is resistant just wouldn't bother to turn up.' Boyns was more inclined to talk about the positive response that these gatherings had prompted. 'It might be that somebody who had been harbouring unhealthy thoughts, somebody who was in the depths of despair but had been keeping these feelings to himself, was now encouraged to seek help, to admit his depression to team-mates in the knowledge that he would get a sympathetic ear. He just needed a prompt, that was all.'

On the one hand, Boyns explained, he was using cricket, namely the clubs – and there were now many – to get his message across. On the other hand, he began to realise that he was tapping into a deep well of potential distress. 'Some club cricketers see their club almost as a family. They yearn for the weekend match as a distraction from the misery of the week. Then they get out for a duck! And matters get worse.' Cricket is very much a game of data – scores, analyses, runs, wickets – as well as results. Your failure – a duck – is there in black and white on the scorecard. The long trudge back to the pavilion with the dreaded 0 going up on the scoreboard is a very public and final humiliation. For people who are already emotionally vulnerable, the setback can be devastating. 'In fact,' Boyns continued, 'cricket is a game of failure.' Don't tell me, I assured him.

There was another point he wanted to stress, one that had not really occurred to me before. 'Yes, cricket is a hobby for the recreational player. But compare it with other hobbies, reading, gardening, stripping old cars, singing in the local church choir, trainspotting, stamp collecting, anything really. You don't have to succeed. You set your own measure of success or failure, and it is a wholly personal judgement. But cricket is not like that. Your failures are always laid bare.' What pressures a professional cricketer has to contend with, I was beginning to understand, were not so different for a club cricketer. It was a sobering thought.

Boyns felt guilt as well as grief at the death of his friend. Could he have been more aware of Alex Miller's inner torment? Could he have helped in any way? What sort of difference might he have made if only he knew? 'So now, through Opening Up Cricket, I *am* making a difference. And I'm doing it in Alex's memory.' His dedication to the cause and the splendid work he and his associates are doing in cricket clubs up and down the country is truly heart-warming … and humbling. Volunteers all, I must add.

Can you give any examples of when you clearly have made a difference? Two sprung to his mind immediately. 'I was told subsequently, following one of our sessions, that one player had been so relieved to realise that he was not alone in his suffering that he booked an appointment with his GP, the first step to getting medical help.' As it happened, this happy outcome provided a bridge between the recreational and the professional game. 'He has now got a contract at one of the counties,' Boyns proudly announced. Following another of the sessions at one club, a chap came up to him and talked about his depression. 'He'd never heard anybody discussing the problem so personally, he told me. Before, he had felt isolated in his misery; now he knew that he was not alone. Other people too were suffering. So, I feel confident that I am getting through to some people.' *You are making a difference.* 'I guess so.'

Is there anybody, I asked him, who would be willing to talk about his experience of Opening Up Cricket? Indeed, there was, I was assured. His name is Matt Jackson, and he is not a team-mate of Boyns at Sefton Park CC but plays for a club in the same neck of the woods. In fact, Jackson not only plays for, but captains, the first XI at Liverpool CC and he was more than willing, eager even, to open up about his mental issues that swirled – and continue to swirl – about this maddening game of ours. Immediately, my memory stirred. *Liverpool CC? Is your home ground in Aigburth?* 'It is,' he replied. *Because Hampshire played Lancashire on that ground sometime in the 1970s. I distinctly recall two things about that match … retreating five yards in the covers when Clive Lloyd came out to bat and the enormous scoreboard.* He laughed. 'Yes, it is rather big.' I am not sure whether it is the tallest scoreboard in the country, but I cannot imagine any *club* scoreboard of superior dimensions. The view from the top, where the scorers sit, over the playing area is stunning.

Jackson has known Boyns for a number of years, playing against each other in the local league. 'I've had depression since my late teens,' he told me, 'and have had anxiety issues on and off ever since.' He got involved in Opening Up Cricket in the early days and helped out with the various physical as well as the mental sessions. 'Seven years ago, I gave up the booze and entered a rehabilitation unit. It was a very difficult time and Opening Up played a huge role when I came out of hospital.' Apart from the assistance given to him personally, the organisation gave him the mental resilience to admit his addiction. 'I was wary of other people's reaction. Still am, if the truth be known. But the fact is, I would never have survived without help.' The key to a stable emotional state, he avers, is routine. If that routine is fractured, he finds himself once again in the downward spiral. Cricket is the centre of his social life in the summer. During the long, dark, winter months, he finds life a struggle.

Did you worry about your personal performances? Would a duck on the Saturday bring down the black clouds of depression to envelop you? 'No, not really. I was always pretty confident I could perform. Besides, I am the captain. My job is to worry about the team's performance, not my own.' The enemy in his case was not fear of failure but drink. He had been picked for the club first XI when he was 14 and of course, drinking at the bar after the game was *de rigueur.* So much for the half of shandy in my youth; nowadays, youngsters are encouraged to drink pints. And not of shandy. This was not a healthy environment, he admitted. 'I just tried to fit in, the way teenagers do,' he pointed out, 'and from there I can trace my later problems.'

The drinking culture has always been present in cricket. The history of the game is littered with drunkards who played the game. Just one of many examples springs readily to my mind. Bobby Peel was suspended by Yorkshire in 1897 for being drunk during a match. Apparently, he was so inebriated that when put on to bowl, he bowled his first ball in the wrong direction. Matt Jackson would not have been alone – not by a long chalk – amongst cricketers who were rather fond of as tipple, many of them famous names. *So, in your case, it was not so much the game of cricket that dismasted you but the social activity surrounding the matches?* 'Yes. We did discuss boozing after the game at the club and whether it was healthy or harmful, but I was always worried about leading the discussions because that meant I would be putting my personal life forward. There we go again … my anxiety reasserting itself.'

All the usual – and to me very familiar – symptoms of depression assailed him in his late teens. He keeps a lid on it, if I can use that expression, with a course of anti-depressants. *I was always told that medication on its own is not the magic arrow. Talking therapy adds another missile to your quiver.* 'That's right. I have good friends around who look out for me. And captaincy has helped because you are forced to look outwards instead of inwards. You have ten other players to look after, rather than becoming wholly introspective. I can honestly say I am enjoying my cricket now as much as I have ever done.'

The work he does for Opening Up Cricket has been therapeutic. He has written a few blogs for them and hopes to do more. 'I am a coach as well as a player,' he said, 'so cricket is my life. And as such, I hope I can help others, not only with their technique but also how to deal with any mental issues that are thrown up when they play the game. Luke Sutton has helped me enormously. Have you ever heard of him?' I assured Jackson that I had. Indeed, much of one chapter in this book is devoted to his work and his influence, I told him.

Change in the club game has been slow, he admits, but it is gathering pace. On one occasion, he led a discussion at a club and was surprised – and gratified – that the topic was hot on social media for days afterwards. 'It's best to talk,' he said, repeating the mantra advanced by so many psychiatrists and counsellors up and down the country. 'But it's very difficult to talk about your mental struggles if you haven't met anyone who has been through the same torment.' *And that is what you do – reassure your listeners that they are not alone.* Like Mark Boyns, he was unwilling to take much credit for that, but I assured him he should.

Whilst watching a recent match in The Cricketer Cup between Old Malvernians and Sherborne Pilgrims (Malvern won, by the way), I fell into conversation with the father of one of the Malvernian players. It transpired that his son had been in No. 5, the House where I was in charge for nine years, but long before his son's time. He had heard that I had written a number of books and that my latest project (this book) was going to be published. When I explained what it was all about, he started to nod vigorously. You must talk to my son, he said; he has suffered from depression brought about by his relationship with the game of cricket and has set up a charity to help cricketers, as well as athletes in a number of sports, who are having mental health issues. I needed no second bidding. At the close of play, I was introduced to Callum Lea, whom I did not know up until this point, and he was enthusiastic about my suggestion of a long chat about his struggles and what he is doing now. In the first flush of victory, deep conversation about depression is not the optimum time for measured reflection, so we agreed to talk at a later date.

That later date was kept, and Callum could not have been more generous with his time. As a young lad, growing up in Staffordshire, he loved his cricket and showed some aptitude in the game. He joined Hinley Cricket Club, played in all the county age groups but at this early stage thoughts of playing professionally were no more than a vague notion in his mind. For the time being, he simply enjoyed the experience of playing with friends, at a reasonably high standard and doing well.

The offer of a cricket scholarship to Malvern College changed all that. The school has an enviable reputation at cricket, and he thrived in the environment, playing in the

College first XI as early on as 13 years of age. 'I thoroughly enjoyed my time at Malvern,' he told me. 'I learnt so much, not just about cricket, though cricket was front and centre of my life, especially in the summer term.' Once term was finished, he turned out for all the Worcestershire age groups during the long summer holidays. 'My best mate was Jack Haynes, who of course made his name at Worcestershire and has now moved to Nottinghamshire, though he still remains my closest friend.' Surrounded as he was by talented and ambitious young cricketers, the dream to play cricket professionally started to take hold and with the examples of others in the College team who were firmly set on the pathway to a professional contract, the dream did not seem fantastical or unobtainable.

At 16, he suffered a stress fracture in his back, which put paid to his bowling, but his batting went from strength to strength. 'I was opening the batting with Jack, and we had several good partnerships in what was a very strong school team.' All seemed to be going smoothly in his life. He was enjoying the educational experience at Malvern and was thriving in the competitive environment of a successful cricket team. 'Had I not gone to Malvern, I would probably have ended up in a grammar school in Wolverhampton, without all the opportunities, both on and off the pitch, that I had at Malvern. I was very grateful for that.'

Problems surfaced when he left school at the age of 18. That summer, he played for the Academy and the county second XI teams at Worcestershire. He had only one thing on his mind – securing a professional contract with the club at the end of the season. Perhaps he put too much pressure on himself. Form deserted him, the runs dried up and his mood darkened. 'I had long periods of low mood. Nothing seemed to be going right.' He felt unable to confide in anyone and made the very valid point that as he was not a contracted player, he was not a member of the Professional Cricketers' Association, therefore unable to avail himself of any help that was available to professional players. He ended the season having failed to make the impression that he had expected and indeed demanded of himself. As he feared, no contract was forthcoming. His dream had been shattered and he was bereft.

Once the season had drawn to a close – this was 2018 – and the bitter pill swallowed and digested, he went on holiday with his parents and at the strong instigation of a friend he sensibly admitted the depth of his despair. His father urged him not to look back at missed opportunities but to plan for the future. What next, he challenged his son. 'This set me thinking,' Callum said. 'If I had fallen by the wayside in my aspirations to turn pro, there must be many more like me, broken with disappointment. And what about other sports? There must be hundreds, possibly thousands, out there who have suffered like me.' For every success story there are countless failures, those who have stumbled over the rubble of their dreams. What support are they getting?

None at all, was his conclusion. So, he set about doing something about it. In January 2020, he set up Sporting Wellness, a charity registered in the UK which seeks to provide free, professional, mental health support for all representative sportsmen and women aged 16 and over. Its success in such a short time has been nothing short of spectacular. 'We now support over 2,500 individuals in 117 different sports, with a 50/50 split between men and women,' he proudly informed me. As I was primarily interested in cricket, I asked him how many of his 2,700 clients were cricketers. 'Over 200.'

He explained what it is that Sporting Wellness offers. It provides free access to its Health Awareness Support Platform, with professional counselling around the clock, seven days a week, support line and a Live Chat facility over the phone, all accessible through a web portal and mobile application. The fact that I, and probably most of my age group, would find the social media jargon somewhat impenetrable does not mean that the tech-savvy generation wouldn't navigate itself easily through the services on offer.

'Not all of our clients are struggling with sport-related problems,' Callum explained. 'There are of course a variety of life issues – redundancy, divorce, debt, substance abuse, illness and so on – that can be the cause of depression and mental health issues, but I would say about 50% are problems directly attributed to sport.' I wondered what Sporting Wellness provided that the PCA did not. First and foremost, he countered, was that the fact that the services offered by the PCA were not available to cricketers who were not professional. Then he drew a deep breath. 'You know, I think there is still this huge stigma attached to depression. Some of the professional cricketers – and a few of them are well-known international players – value the absolute confidentiality which we can guarantee. In the back of their minds is the fear that their struggles might leak out.' He made the very valid point that going public with mental health problems is very much a personal choice. Often the individual does not want to admit to his 'weakness' until after his career has ended. Furthermore, Callum reminded me that his services were free. 'Not everybody can afford private health care and as you know, mental health is woefully underfunded in the NHS.'

As the services were free, I wondered how on earth Sporting Wellness was funded. Purely by charitable donations, through the usual channels, such as Just Giving and Give As You Live Online. There are numerous fund-raising activities countrywide. A latest one was a charity ball, held at Molineux, home to Wolverhampton Wanderers FC. He has four full volunteers acting as trustees (one of whom is his father) and two part-time employees (one of whom is himself). He has entered into partnership with numerous universities, colleges and clubs – but sadly – inexplicably – not one county cricket club has taken up his offer. This upsets him. 'I reached out to them a while back and had no response. Particularly disappointing is the fact that I have tried to contact the ECB several times about helping the county age groups and Academy players and, like the counties, their silence has been strange.' His guess is that possibly the ECB and the counties do not want to be seen soliciting outside support. If so, this is reprehensible. Not for the first time, I hear so many 'mission statements' of cricket clubs affirming their support for the mental health of their players that do not suit much practical action to the word. A lot has been done to remove the stigmatisation of depression but not enough, says Callum; much more work needs to be done.

How are you now, Callum? 'In a much better place. I think I'm managing my mental health more successfully. And this charity I have set up has given me a focus in my life that seemed to become cloudy towards the end of my career.' It seems perverse to talk of an end-of-career about a young man in his early twenties, but as he pointed out, he is not alone in this regard. It has been a fact of life for many 'failures', those who never made it in the professional game, ever since Victorian times. He no longer plays, even recreationally. 'I found it difficult to drop down a level from where I once was and wanted to be.' He has reached a stage of acceptance of this state of affairs; he is still closely involved in the game, even if his playing days, it seems, are over. 'I'm happy with my relationship with cricket, even if it is now once removed.' He works as an agent for Quantum Sport, which acts for cricketers to source overseas contracts, particularly in the Indian Premier League (IPL). Among their clientele can be numbered David Willey, Mark Wood, Will Jacks, Mark Stoneman, Jack Leach, Jamie Porter, Jamie Smith and a host of other English professionals. 'The first client I signed was Will Smeed from Somerset, a great friend and the one I most closely work with.'

If he had his time again, he says, he would simply enjoy playing cricket to a high standard in his childhood and teenage years without putting so much pressure on himself, 'without fixating on doing it for a career'. As a consequence, he found the environment on the fringes of the professional game too stressful and did not enjoy his time at the Worcestershire Academy and playing in the second XI. 'What I want to encourage is an understanding of how crucial it is to have a balanced, diversified identity that isn't wrapped up in cricket.' It is a noble endeavour of his and one can only wish him and Sporting Wellness well. Nothing like the help he is giving to cricketers of today was available to previous generations, those who felt they failed and couldn't get over it.

'What do they know of cricket
who only cricket know?'

(CLR James,
cricket historian and political activist)

Conclusion

So, What is the Answer?

THE QUESTION I posed – to myself as much as to anybody else – at the beginning of this book was this: is cricket to blame or are cricketers, by their very nature, more susceptible to clinical depression? After reading untold articles and several books, having interviewed a number of former players and having examined my own experience, including the opinion and counsel of my psychiatrists and psychotherapists, it might be assumed that I had come to some sort of conclusion to my survey of the evidence.

The short answer is that I do not believe there *is* one answer, at least not one that can be called a solution to the problem, to the dilemma. Scientists love a verifiable explanation; they deal in certainty, in proven fact. Therefore, it must be a cause of some dismay, frustration even, that science has thrown up no absolute verdict on the cause, and the effective treatment, of depression. If my research has told me one thing, it is that no two cases are alike. Individual experience varies; no one size fits all. Some of my subjects blame cricket and the strains it puts on the human psyche. Others accept that quite possibly their own nature lends itself to bouts of melancholia. The rest just don't know, their bleakness is inexplicable, and they drive themselves nuts trying to uncover a reason. In the end, what goes on in anyone's mind is unknowable. At times, what goes on in our own mind is baffling enough.

Nonetheless, it is true that a good number of cricketers suffer from the affliction. For affliction is what it undeniably is. I have lost count of the number of times I have been told that depression is an illness, just as valid as heart disease, diabetes, cancer ... or even a broken leg. The mind is broken, I was told, but we cannot put it in plaster to let it set. It is not visible; you do not need crutches to get about, but you need a crutch of another sort to function as a human being. It's nothing to be ashamed of; it's good to talk. We have left those uninformed days behind us.

But we haven't, not really. There is still a stigma attached to an admission of depression, of mental weakness, of an inability to cope with the pressures of succeeding, or trying to succeed, at this frustrating game of ours. Proof of this, I think, is that so few current players and former players still involved in the game have been willing to come forward and let me interview them. They are entitled to their anonymity – and I respect that absolutely. But it does suggest that they perceive their malady – or at least fear that their employers might perceive it to be so – as a sign of weakness. And what you must *never* do in any contest between individuals (and as we know, cricket is a team game incorporating head-to-head confrontation) is to show weakness. Perhaps we have not come as far as we believe.

I cannot pretend that I am happy with the state of play after all these hours of work. I would have expected to be much nearer an answer to the conundrum of cricket and the black dog; but the winning total feels as far away as ever. It seems that the bowlers have got the better of me and I cannot score a run, and that the umpires are on the point of putting me out of misery and pulling up the stumps.

Is depression just a state of mind? Depression *is* just a state of mind, just as a broken leg is a state of bone, that heart disease is a state of heart, that diabetes is a state of pancreas. The problem is with the use of the word 'just', for it suggests that something is simply – only – no more than what it describes, nothing greatly to worry about ('just a bad day at the office'). Perhaps the label 'depression' is misleading. We should never again, I suggest, say we are depressed when we are simply in a low mood, the cause of which is clear to us. A string of low scores would put anyone in a low mood; the problem occurs when the dejection spirals into a semi-permanent state of negativity and self-abasement. That is when help must be sought and sympathetically given. Cricket spares no one, as Jonathan Trott said. Men have gone mad for less.

The problem, brought to the forefront of public awareness by the Trescothick book, has possibly been elbowed aside by the gathering controversy surrounding contact sport and its connection to the early onset of dementia. Constant heading of a ball is the prime suspect in football. Five of the England team that won the World Cup in 1966 have died of dementia: Ray Wilson, Jack Charlton, Nobby Stiles, Martin Peters and Bobby Charlton. Over 200 former rugby players are suing the Rugby Football Union for dereliction of care, as they have subsequently been diagnosed with early-onset dementia, following multiple cases of concussion. The collisions in the game nowadays are enough to make even strong men wince. The National Football League in the US is currently battling with its own crisis of head injuries … and they wear helmets! But depression and elite level sport has not gone away. Owen

Farrell, the rugby player, has recently stepped back from playing for England to 'protect his mental health'. The snooker player, Ronnie O'Sullivan, has had his very public struggles with mental health. The swimmer, Michael Phelps, fell into 'a state of major depression' after every Olympics. Serena Williams revealed that she had been battling depression after winning Wimbledon in 2010. Naomi Osaka, seeded No. 2, retired from the French Open in 2021 after the first round, saying she was suffering from depression. Paul Pogba said he suffered bouts of depression while playing for Manchester United under Jose Mourinho. Cricket is not alone.

Yet cricketers do seem to be more susceptible to depression than other elite sportsmen and women. Many of the possible reasons have already been examined. The high incidence might be attributed to the tendency of players to acute self-examination in a game which gives ample opportunity for analysis, scrutiny and introspection. Striving for perfection – or aiming to avoid imperfection – is a potent driver of disappointment and ultimately self-abnegation. As ever, Shakespeare put it better than most:

> *'The fault, dear Brutus, is not in*
> *our stars, but in ourselves.'*
>
> (Cassius, *Julius Caesar*)

We are not ever going to stop playing cricket, with all its capability to drive us to distraction, so we had better prepare ourselves, and those who come after us, to deal with its pitfalls, to put in place strategies and support networks for both prevention and management of the illness. But in the end – and this is only my personal view – the motivation to cope must come from within. I'm reminded of the oft-quoted judgement of experts in the field of addiction; no cure can be effected unless a) the patient understands and accepts the scale of his or her problem and b) willingly embraces the means – no matter how difficult and painful – by which remedy can be achieved.

As the two finalists take to Centre Court to do battle for the Wimbledon crown, they will see inscribed just above their heads these words as they exit the Members' Lounge:

> 'If you can meet with Triumph and Disaster
> And treat those two imposters just the same … '

Whenever I read those words (not that I have ever played in the Wimbledon Championships!), I wonder if Jimmy Connors, John McEnroe. Pete Sampras, Martina Navratilova, Serena Williams, Novak Djokovic and the rest ever bothered to read it, and if they did, what was their reaction – a contemptuous shrug? Winners simply don't think like that.

Rudyard Kipling has fallen out of favour these days, mainly because of his perceived jingoism and imperialism, but I think some of his words still resonate down the years. There are other lines from that poem *If* that might – or should – strike a chord with those of us cricketers who have struggled with their 'mental health', that catch-all term that undoubtedly embraces depression.

Keep busy, never give in and try to maintain a sense of proportion. Stay focussed on what is important to you and your ambition. If they diverge, reconsider your position. Look in the mirror, not out of the window. Share your worst fears with someone. It might just be the saving of you.

Cricketers die twice. I guess it's a case, and always has been, of how we fare in the second innings.

Acknowledgements

WHAT PROMPTED you to write this book, I have been asked. It came about by chance. Before the idea was planted in my head, I had never given the possibility a moment's thought. In fact, early on in my battles with depression, I would have run a mile if anybody had suggested I write a book about it. I *hated* self-analysis, talking about myself and my inner feelings. That was how we were brought up, stiff upper lip and all that. We were expected to 'man up'; after all, worse things happen at sea, as my aged aunt was fond of saying, usually apropos of nothing. I remember vividly a football match at school. I was pretty good at the game and captained the first XI. I had been brutally hacked down by one of the cloggers in the opposing team and lay crumpled in a heap in the mud. My father, on the touchline, bellowed, 'Get up! Get up! You're down to ten men!' He wasn't necessarily being unsympathetic. He had played football in his youth. He knew that occasionally you get fouled and that a badly timed tackle can hurt. That goes with the territory. Unless your leg is broken, you can get up and soon run off the niggle. Football is played by men, not cissies. It was an instructive lesson, one that was to stand me in good stead throughout my cricket career and throughout life, in fact. His generation had been through a war; there was no time, and little sympathy, for self-indulgent navel-gazing.

The trouble was, over the course of many years of my treatment for depression, I had to unlearn this life's lesson. Keeping things bottled up was not a good thing, I was told; the brain will overheat and eventually blow a gasket. A problem shared is a problem halved. It's good to talk. It's OK not to feel OK. All the cliches from the mental health playbook were lobbed in my direction. It was a while before I stopped spilling them deliberately. I was not being obtuse or obstructive; it was just that old habits die hard. Even now, I am not very good at coming clean about how I really feel, but I am getting better … I think.

One of the possible side-effects of electro-convulsive therapy (ECT) is that there might be some short-term memory loss. When making a speech to the Cheltenham Cricket Society, I bore this in mind during my preamble to the audience. If I can't remember a name of a player, please forgive me, I said, and don't be shy at reminding me. As it happened, for a few seconds, I had struggled to remember the name of the Australian umpire who had given Tony Greig out lbw first ball – on television – off my bowling. 'Bill Alley!' they chorused. I then explained the possible reason for this momentary lapse in my memory and gave a potted version of my travails with depression and the treatment to which I had been subjected. The rest of my presentation passed off without any further alarms and excursions and was well received, I thought.

Afterwards, there was a queue of people coming up to congratulate me, not on my speech, but on my 'bravery' for laying bare the circumstances of my illness, something that is still regarded in some circles as taboo, not talked about and, more often than not, swept under the carpet.

I was dumbfounded. I did not consider myself 'brave' at all. Bravery is having to face Michael Holding and Jeff Thomson, I quipped (which I had).

One in the queue I recognised instantly when he opened his mouth. He has the most mellifluous tones to his voice of anybody I have ever listened to, perfect, I would think, for the job of the PA announcer at Lord's or the Oval (which he does, as a matter of fact). He had earlier in his career worked alongside Lord MacLaurin in the fledgling England and Wales Cricket Board (ECB) as their marketing guru. He had been immensely helpful to me, when writing Ian MacLaurin's biography, with insights of life in an organisation at a very exciting time of its infancy. Terry Blake is his name and next time you are at a Test match at either of those historic grounds, listen out for him and you will understand what I mean.

He confided in me that he is a fellow sufferer, 'a recovering depressive', as he put it. He then planted the seed of an idea that grew into a project which has now seen the light of day as a published book. 'This is currently a hot topic,' he said. 'If we can get cricketers on board who have publicly admitted to problems with their mental health, your writing about it will help spread the good word and probably help you too.' Thus, sprung a partnership and a friendship, to our great mutual benefit. My citation at the front of the book, dedicating it to Terry Blake, says it all.

There are others to whom I am grateful for giving of their time and their opinion so generously. I list them in no other order than that which they appear in the book: David Frith, John Barclay, Luke Sutton, Jeremy Snape, Andrew Wingfield Digby, Graeme Fowler, Barry Richards, Dudley Owen-Thomas, David Nash, Ian Thomas, Huw Turbervill, Mark Boyns, Matt Jackson and Callum Lea

My wife proof-read the manuscript and was helpful with corrections, suggestions and clear judgement.

Lastly, I should like to extend my grateful thanks to all those at Pitch Publishing, in particular Duncan Olner, Bruce Talbot and Jane Camillin.